A HITCHHIKER'S GUIDE TO UNDERSTANDING ORGANISATIONS

And stuff to do to enhance and enjoy them!

DAVID PARIS

This book is dedicated to my family and friends but especially to my beautiful daughter Gabrielle. She has triumphed over every adversity she has faced since birth, and wonderfully retained the sense of joy and enthusiasm for life, and generosity of spirit towards others that are humbling and so enviable.

A Hitchhiker's Guide To Understanding Organisations
© David Paris (The Paris Family Trust) 2024

ISBN: 978-1-7638506-0-6 (Paperback)

Cover Design: David Paris
Format and Typeset: Clark & Mackay
Self-Published by David Paris with assistance from Clark & Mackay

Proudly printed in Australia by Clark & Mackay

CONTENTS

PROLOGUE

I'd like to thank Douglas Adams as the inspiration for both the title of this work and its underlying structure. It is a journey, in which you will randomly come across individuals, concepts, theories, authors, anecdotes, observations, case studies and other miscellaneous stuff. I hope you will find it an interesting journey, at least in parts, maybe intriguing, probably at times surprising as well as illuminating. I hope it will be rewarding, in that you will have enjoyed the journey and the experience and got a few glimpses into how you can open doors into understanding organisations. I must add that this all had its genesis while I was in hospital following an urgent lifesaving operation. It was about midnight, and I just could not get to sleep. Suddenly my drugged brain went into overdrive and a voice said "You have to write a book, a book on understanding organisations and you have to write it your way!" About thirty minutes later, the voice told me the title of the book. I started the next day. I've used pseudonyms only where I felt it necessary to protect the guilty. I also apologise for all the I's. It is biographical!

Biography hazard ahead, exit Wormhole to page 9 or x.

Before proceeding, I should probably give a brief overview of an eclectic career that took me on my journey of discovery on which I'm taking the reader. Following time in Australia as a Jackaroo and aviator in the Australian Navy I commenced a career in commerce with management roles in major corporates in the following fields: toiletries, tobacco, finance, insurance, pharmaceuticals and engineering. I then did a mature age university degree in commerce. I did well, won scholarships and was invited to become a university lecturer. I accepted and then got on the academic roller coaster completing three more degrees in education, behavioural sciences and organisational research. Over these years I lectured in and undertook consulting assignments in Australia, UK, USA, Canada, Middle East, Indonesia and Singapore. I also started three successful companies in finance, coffee and tourism and floated a technical company on the stock exchange. I fundamentally owed this all to my great preparatory school education and thus to my maternal grandfather who I never met! This journey is biographical but not chronological it follows some of the important experiences and events as they come to mind that led to my understanding organisations. While my journey was largely in Australia my years overseas confirmed the experiences could have been in any country, subject only to cultural variables.

MY EARLY LIFE

A little more about me, the navigator!

I was born in conditions of significant poverty in the East End of London, so I am technically a Cockney, born within the sound of Bow Bells. My father was at war, and we shared a room in a charity home, that was later destroyed in the blitz. My mother told me she had to pawn her engagement ring to put food on the table. The interest rate was one shilling per pound per week needed to redeem it. I calculated that this was an interest rate of 260% per annum. Usury in the extreme! Quite how we survived I don't know, as I was evacuated from London at different times during the war to Scotland, Morecombe and Cornwall.

One day at the age of seven, I was suddenly told I was off to an exclusive preparatory boarding school in Berkshire. I was much later to discover that this was by means of a bursary from St Paul's School in London, and thanks to my grandfather, who was chief stonemason at St Paul's Cathedral, and whose headstone is in the crypt. This was my Eliza Doolittle moment. Five years later I was unrecognisable as the guttersnipe the headmistress had once called me. I've loved that word ever since.

I had a classical English education in languages, literature and each field of mathematics.

From the age of seven, I was reading De Maupassant, Wilkie Collins, Shakespeare, Orczy, Dickens, Kipling and many others. Like Eliza, my voice and accent became indistinguishable from those of the so-called public school educated upper class. I was also a chorister doing solos as a boy soprano in our local church. I even became head boy based on my social and academic achievements. My problem now was going home, as I was so radically different from my family and friends in speech, manners, education and interests. I was constantly being told "now we aren't good enough for you". Within my family's peer group, no one aspired to do anything other than to follow their parent's careers. To even think of doing so was considered uppity or self-important and arrogant. This is of course an example of a cultural problem that we find equally in organisations. With the changes I had undergone I no longer fitted into my family's peer group. In organisations this frequently occurs when staff have been sent on behavioural training programs or undertaken further studies such as MBA's. There are often what are termed re-entry problems, as the individuals have changed expectations of the organisation and their role in it. In one research study on MBA graduates over 50% had left their organisation within twelve months. Some organisations I know of recognised this, and as a result ceased supporting and financing staff study programs. Unfortunately, and more unfortunately as it is not recognised, the same re-entry problem also happens in families. It is not uncommon for marriage breakdown to occur after either one or both spouses attend behavioural training courses or tertiary education studies. The reasons are essentially the same as those in organisations. Changed needs or expectations.

My 11 plus exam was a romp and I went to a great Grammar School into the top form. But I was still expected to pull my weight at home, and from the age of 11 held down three jobs. From these I paid the 22 shillings rent on our council house and shared the food bill. What was left was mine. After five years I completed my GCE exams and left school to work. Extending my schooling and going to university was simply not an option.

I was always adventurous, doing cycling and camping trips to dozens of places, riding as much as 120 miles in a day. I was also a member of the Worldwide Club reading every magazine from cover to cover of amazing adventures in Canada, South America, New Guinea and Australia. I was to discover 40 years later that they were all written by a gentleman living in Somerset who had never been outside England in his life. Yet, it was this magazine and its great stories that led me to leave England and head to Australia!

I got my first job as a laboratory technician in Regent Street Polytechnic. I enjoyed it, but I looked around grey London and thought not for me, plus I wanted to escape my parents and the class society of England. I tried first to go to Canada, but they had no schemes for minors. One lunch time I walked to Australia House in The Strand and asked about emigrating. They said, "We want people like you," and so, without informing my parents, I supplied my school results, got references, had a medical and within three weeks I'd been accepted. My main memory is of my medical. After the usual checks of eyes, ears and etcetera, I was told to drop my trousers and jocks. The young female doctor then took my testicles in her hand and said "cough"! In a state of semi-shock, I said "what do you want me to do?", and sternly but with a half-smile she said "COUGH" and I complied! The first of many such future demands! At 16 I was a minor, so had to get parental consent to leave England. I took the paperwork home and told my mother that I wanted to go to Australia, and she had to sign to let me go. She asked me if I was serious. I said yes, so she signed and a month later I sailed from Southampton to start a new career in Australia. The voyage was a great adventure. We went through a huge storm in the Bay of Biscay with massive seas breaking over the bow with the screws screaming as they came out of the ocean. Then, after Gibraltar, we sailed to Naples. Here, with, a friend I'd made, we went by horse drawn carriage from port to city being dropped in what turned out to be the red-light district, like Soho in London. Here we had our first wood fired pizza and then, feeling very mature sixteen-year-olds, we headed back to the ship. It was from then on, a wondrous 30-day voyage with many adventures, but there are two incidents indelibly imprinted in my memory. The first was as we cruised along the African coast, with the sun blazing and smoke drifting up from thatched dwellings, I was taken by the sheer beauty at that moment in time. Impulsively, I took off a gold signet ring I'd been given for my sixteenth birthday and threw it into the millpond surface of the mediterranean. The sun glinted on it as it sank below the surface. That act and the African coast is as vivid now as it was on the day. The second was in Singapore, which at the time had open drains alongside dusty gravel roads, and where I went exploring by myself. I needed to relieve myself and went into a large white building that I was later to discover was the famous Raffles Hotel. I entered the men's toilet relieved myself, and then as I went to button up, a hand with a small towel delicately dabbed my manhood before it got tucked away. I was too stunned to say anything but thought what kind of a society it was when that elderly lady's job was to sit in a toilet providing that service to men.

From Singapore we arrived in West Australia, surrounded as we approached the harbour by a wonderful pod of whales. Following a shore trip, we left to sail around the coast to Sydney where we disembarked. I then went to a farm outside Sydney to learn the fundamentals of farm life and was then put on a train to travel 400 miles to start my new career as a jackaroo. Jackaroos are trainee station managers. In Australia, stations are large rural properties with some far exceeding 1,000,000 hectares. This was the best decision of my life, and I had a vertical learning curve. In no time at all I could drive cars, trucks, and tractors. I could plough, sow and harvest crops. I could ride stock horses, round up sheep, cattle and wild running horses on the property. I could milk cows, make butter and butcher sheep. I could remove tails and castrate lambs by the hundreds. I could shear sheep, dehorn rams, fell trees, turn them into fence posts, erect the fences and build wool sheds. I learned more skills in 12 months than I'd learned in my preceding 16 years. My best and really close mates were Laddie, a border collie and Darkie, my beautiful horse I rode every day. Then after 18 months I saw an advertisement to join the Australian Navy, to be an aviator in the Fleet Air Arm. I was a successful applicant joining the other 15 from across Australia. I did all my naval training, then flying training, successfully soloing and loving all the aerobatics as well as the adventures with my amazing colleagues drawn from all walks of life. Our transport was a vintage Austin 8 convertible, called the iron mistress, that could carry seven, with two sitting astride the bonnet giving hand signals of when to turn!

Unfortunately, I had some major arguments with my instructor, who was an alcoholic, and who deemed me only suitable to be an observer, a navy navigator, and I left for the UK to train in Cornwall with the Royal Navy. The Qantas flight in a Super Constellation took three days and cost half my annual salary! In Cornwall I had a fantastic time at work and play. We were often, illegally, flying and navigating at wave height under the bows of ships in the English Channel. The epitome of flying skills was to just flick the top of a wave with your propeller! We regularly flew to France, where a remarkable number of aircraft had engine failures forcing you to land. Miraculousy, after purchasing numerous bottles of French wine, the aircraft became airworthy and we took off to return to base, without going through customs! The most fantastic time was undergoing high altitude selection tests. These included being shot up in ejection seats, crashing into a deep pool strapped in an aircraft and having to escape without panicking, being dumped in a wild sea in small inflatable lifeboats, and to be rescued by helicopter. The hairiest times were doing an unstable spin in a Venom fighter from 50,000 feet and pulling out just prior to crashing, and being explosively decompressed in a pressure chamber, simulating ejection at 30,000 feet, plus so much more! One of the greatest fun times of my life! At the same time, I was exploring Cornwall and ended up managing a farming property, part of 1000 year old Bochym Manor. This was on my weekends, when I was milking cows, ploughing, fencing and using all my jackaroo skills. I loved it and was asked if I'd be their full-time manager but declined due to my navy career! However, it seemed I was doomed in the navy, as just prior to graduation I got a serious sporting injury, was flown back to Australia, hospitalised for 3 months and evaluated as unfit to fly. With hindsight, this was probably fortunate as it led to me having a far more varied and interesting life. A sliding door moment that took me into the fields of commerce, academia and consulting.

THE ORGANISATIONAL SPACESHIP

At the controls are the leadership team so let's have a look at leadership, culture and managing. These three are inextricably intertwined in organisations with each influencing and influenced by the others. They also have the most profound effect on organisational behaviour and performance.

It could be worthwhile here having a quick review of the principal differences between leading and managing.

Leading is principally about vision, inspiration, influence and trust. Leaders create a vision for the future that others can share, desire and believe can be realised by following and trusting the leader. The leader then must empower and motivate the followers to take the actions required to attain the desired future. Wonderful examples of such leaders with a vision would be Nelson Mandela and democracy, Martin Luther King Jr and racial equality and Steve Jobs with technical beauty and innovation. Examples of authenticity and integrity would include The Dalai Lama, Malala Yousafzai fighting the Taliban and advocating for girl's education. Examples of empowerment and development would include Eleanor Roosevelt with human rights and social justice and Bill Gates giving employees freedom take risks and innovate. As with groups and teams, leading and leadership are not innately good. No leader is perfect. They have flaws and can make mistakes. The history of countries, religions and corporations abounds with examples of leading and leadership that has resulted in the death of millions, destruction of nations, liquidation of companies and losses by millions of individuals believing in and trusting others and the future they have promised.

I recall being visited one night at home by four owners of very successful businesses who invited me to go with them to an investment seminar. Based on the answers to a few questions I'd asked, I declined, saying it sounded like a pyramid scheme. I always remember the response of the proponent. It was "condemnation without investigation is the height of ignorance".

The following day I got a phone call from one of the businessmen whose company employed over 500 persons. He told me two of his business colleagues were going to sign up and would I come with him to dissuade them. He was a truly hardheaded person but told me that he had to keep saying to himself that there is no Santa Claus, there is no Santa Claus, such was the power of the proponent's oratory. The adage "if it sounds too good to be true then it almost certainly is" should be heeded by all, yet every year we hear of so many who failed to heed. To reiterate, the one essential thing required to be a leader are followers. This a fundamental difference from managers. In so many organisations you see or hear people describe themselves as a leader or the leader. In many or possibly most cases they are not as they have no followers, rather they just have subordinates, and so at best are managers. In my experience where people labour under the illusion that they are a leader, they are also poor managers. This is simply because they tend to resort to control where subordinate behaviours do not meet their leadership expectations of what that behaviour should be!

Rather than have followers, managers or supervisors will have subordinates and the authority associated with their role to give subordinates orders. It's important to remember that the authority is given to the role and not to the individual, but that's not how most managers perceive it. They seem to think they personally have the authority. In an ideal world we'd like all managers to be good leaders, but this is the exception. Managers relying on authority to control subordinates, as many do, are likely to have disaffected subordinates who work to rule, are unwilling to question questionable orders, who do not exercise initiative and are ready to leave at the first good opportunity. I had a significant consulting job for a remotely located major gold mining company experiencing very high staff turnover. They wanted to try and establish the cause of this costly loss of staff to other mining companies. To do this, through networking and associates in other comparable mining companies, I was able to establish that salaries, bonuses, accommodation and other conditions and facilities provided were only matched by one other company in the industry. I was also able to establish that the average staff turnover rate in the other companies was half of that in the client. Based on your experiences I'm sure as readers you already have the answer. It did prove to be the way frontline supervisors were treating subordinates. Not only were they relying on authority, but it was fear based with abusive language, threats of the worst shift patterns or dismissal. This behaviour trumped all the great pay and conditions the company offered! The resolution of this widespread problem required significant cultural and behavioural change, not throughout the company but simply at the frontline level. A program was implemented to change the culture. An interesting outcome was that many of the supervisors or frontline managers, with the aberrant behaviours, were repeating behaviours they had been subject to. It was an organisational version of the expression "the sins of the father are visited upon the children". With the intervention achieving cultural and behavioural change the reduction in staff losses was progressively brought down to a turnover rate comparable to the best in the industry. I'll add here just two basic but valuable leader or manager guidelines that I have followed and are easily remembered. From author and poet Rudyard Kipling, I have six honest serving men they taught me all I knew. Their names were what and why and when and how and where and who. From my navy time I got the 7 P's. Prior preparation and planning prevents piss poor performance. And it does!

Let's look at to some organisational vandals we need to avoid!

From Apex to Nadir – A Pharmaceutical Company Story

This is a story about someone who absolutely did not understand organisations.

This American company, the largest private company of its kind in the world, was headquartered in Sydney and had been established by Bob Peters, who was the managing director.

The staff amenities were amazing, even including a nine-hole golf- course. He was a great leader and great manager, a relatively rare combination. His emphasis was on his staff working as a client-focussed collegiate team, with minimum bureaucracy and management intervention, and with innovation and initiative encouraged at every level. He was respected by everyone from the storeman to major clients. Unfortunately for us, his success was such that he got promoted to head up South-East Asia and the Pacific.

His replacement was a manager named Rob T. He was from the UK and a totally different kettle of fish in just about every way. He was authoritarian, arrogant, a bully and a boor. It was a classic case of "it's my way or the highway". No-one respected him. He instituted policies and practices that negatively affected both staff and clients. As he sensed the resistance and disaffection in staff and clients, he increasingly micromanaged every aspect of the organisation.

This led to a dramatic change in organisational culture and behaviour. We rapidly started losing clients and staff. From being zero, staff turnover went through the roof. In every case, we were told that the company did not need people like them. I went to see him and said I'd like to undertake a university course in management. His response was to say, "There is nothing you need to know about managing a company that you can't learn from me." As all I had learned was how to destroy a fantastic company, I resigned. As with other departing staff, it turned out that the company did not need people like me. I followed the company progress to see what happened. Within two years, with increasing financial losses, the company ceased its staffed operation in Australia, and sold its premises, with ongoing operations continuing through an agency network only.

Due to Bob Peters' foresight, the profits on the sale of the factory site and staff nine-hole golf course, with industrial real estate having boomed in price, far exceeded the profits from the entire Australian operation.

The question I had then and still have today is, "How did the organisation not see the damage being wrought before it was fatally injured?" I've had the same question in many organisations since then. There can be a variety of reasons for this from nepotism, to fear of retaliation, or unwillingness to accept responsibility for the errors in judgement.

Culturally Naïve – A Tobacco Company Story

This is a story about how self-proclaimed experts totally misread a market and its culture.

From as early as the 1880s, the tobacco industry in Australia was dominated, virtually to monopoly status, by WD & HO Wills, a subsidiary of Imperial Tobacco. As with many monopolies they considered themselves impregnable. Wills management felt little need to innovate or market their brands, feeling they could just maintain the status quo enjoying monopoly profits.

Suddenly, out of the blue, a new tobacco company invaded the Australian market like a blitzkrieg, with new brands, exciting advertising, sporting orientation and popular figureheads. This company was Rothmans. The company was founded by Louis Rothman in 1890, as a small kiosk on Fleet Street in London. In 1900, Rothman opened a small showroom in Pall Mall, from which he launched his famous Pall Mall cigarette brand. His reputation was such that King Edward VII granted Rothman a royal warrant in 1905.

From this start Rothmans saw substantial growth in brands such as Dunhill, Rothmans and Peter Stuyvesant and entered geographical markets outside the United Kingdom including South Africa. Rothmans invaded Australia in the early 1970s, with its initial brands of Rothmans and Peter Stuyvesant. Rothmans sold itself as the man's cigarette, with marketing based on local sports and the great outdoors. Stuyvesant, an all-white cigarette was targeted at women and the more sophisticated sports and travelling public as "the passport to international pleasure". Then came Rothman's breakthrough hit, with Winfield brand. It was promoted by Paul Hogan. Paul Hogan was a comedian creating and acting in hugely popular comedy shows and had superstar status.

These brands and marketing massively impacted Wills and Imperial Tobacco. To give some idea of Winfield's success, after British American Tobacco acquired Rothmans in 1999, in 2004 alone, they shipped 853 billion Winfield cigarettes. But I digress. In 1964 Gallagher International, a major UK tobacco company decided to try to enter the Australian market.

I applied for and got the role of marketing manager and was the only Australian in a management role. All other senior managers were British to the core. I was then introduced to the launch product as well as the advertising and promotion that was proposed for it. The name was Edinburgh and the packaging not dissimilar to Rothman's Stuyvesant, primarily white with a blue and red logo. The television campaign, however, blew me out of the water. They showed a series of different settings, such as gracious lounge rooms or beautiful country gardens. In these was featured an elegant and somewhat effeminate James Condon, unknown in Australia. He was wearing a reefer jacket and a cravat, anathema in Australia, and was drawing on his Edinburgh while engaged in conversation with equally elegant friends.

This advertising was so reminiscent of class-based English society, and so totally and utterly out of place in Australia and out of touch with Australians, that I couldn't believe what I was seeing. However, the English executives loved it. Despite this, putting my reservations aside, I headed off with a sales promotion team of representatives, all athletes in different sports, to promote the Edinburgh brand across New South Wales, covering pubs, the major club networks such as RSL, leagues, football, cricket, lifesaving, golf, sailing and so on. This was 1964 and, through a friend, I met and took the The Beatles and Brian Epstein sailing on Pittwater, and even had The Beatles smoking Edinburgh cigarettes on TV, quite a coup. I also discovered whisky and coke when I sat on a bedroom floor in the Sheraton hotel with Ringo Starr and we attacked a litre of Black Label and two litres of Coke!

Everywhere we went our team was received well, and we handed out tens of thousands of samples. The cigarettes were enjoyed, and we got positive feedback, but the criticism of the TV ads was universal, with the most common comment being, "Who is the poof you are using in your ads. Is he a Pommie or something?" We were away for some weeks and, when I finally got back to Sydney I sat down with the English executives and told them how and why our TV campaign was a disaster and needed drastic changes.

I was put in my place in no uncertain terms and told, "We know how to market tobacco products and cigarettes. You do not." So, I resigned on the spot. When they asked me why I said because this company has no future. They were gobsmacked at the temerity of this young 25-year-old telling them they were going to fail. I left, with them still shaking their heads in disbelief at my arrogance. The company lasted not much more than a year. Edinburgh disappeared, and they folded their tents and decamped back to the UK, never to be seen again. No doubt they told stories of the barbaric, uncouth, and uncultured Australians they had had to deal with. It was a complete and utter failure, grounded in such ignorance or arrogance, that they just failed to accept the fact that Australia's culture was so very different from that in England.

A Mining Company Story

This is an example of an organisational sociopath: I was asked to join a major iron ore producing company in Western Australia. The role was supposed to be one that employed my academic and practical business skills in organisational development. I was to report to the General Manager. He was responsible for the entire operation of the port and ore loading facility, as well as the mine sites scattered over a few thousand square kilometres. Let's call him RM. He turned out to be another Rob T from the pharmaceutical company. He was authoritarian, arrogant, a bully and a boor. Again, with him it was again a case of "my way or the highway". We were aiming to rapidly double our production tonnage, and were seeking an additional 1,500 employees on the various mine sites.

The weekly so-called management meetings were a farce. They just amounted to RM. telling everyone what he wanted done and how. No one ever questioned anything he said. Everyone knew that would result in you going on his hit list for early dismissal. It was management by fear. In that climate, all our good managers and superintendents were leaving to join other companies. This was seen by RM as good riddance to bad rubbish. I raised this issue at a senior management meeting to be told by one "if they don't like it, they can fuck off". This while we were desperately trying to recruit our 1500 new staff!

One day, after a death on a mining site the mine superintendent, a great manager, closed the site. It was his prerogative and was absolutely company policy.

However, RM was furious that this action had been taken without his consent, arguing that it was not needed. The mine superintendent was then put on RM's hit list and was effectively harassed until he quit. As with Rob T, RM claimed we didn't need people like him in our company. This was clearly code for "I only want yes men in my company".

I got on well with the mine superintendent and I was delighted when the person we didn't need, was snapped up by another mining company as CEO with a million-dollar annual package. His package was now some 400% more than RM's. At least at times RM acted as a manager, even though a not very good one, and had respect from some quarters. However, he decided to have a relationship with a staff member, one who was well known on site. This person was then moved into an office in the senior management complex and, worse still, appointed to a senior role in that office.

This is an example of management decision making we never see in textbooks. In all the books on management motivation and management decision making, I've never seen a chapter headed The Role of Love, Lust and Lechery, yet I've seen it somewhere in almost every organisation I've ever worked with! As no doubt have you!

In RM's case his actions met with head-shaking and a total loss of credibility throughout the operation, along with loss of respect. Shortly after this episode and having had several disagreements with RM, he promoted me to a non-role. It was due to become redundant, so as had so many others, I left the company.

Later, I heard that top management had finally recognised the cause of us losing all our best managers and superintendents, and RM had to find himself a new job. In this case, as is the case in many large companies, the sheer size and extent of their income and resources, allow them to easily recover from poor management. There have been examples in BHP, the largest mining company in the world, where the CEO made investment decisions that cost the company billions. Despite this they are usually "let go" with a golden parachute, often due to poorly structured contracts. Shades of Qantas, and chainsaw Jack, covered later. There is frequently the question of how was the CEO or senior manager left in their role for so long? There are many possible reasons for this as alluded to earlier. They include contractual obligations, and a weak board, reluctant to admit failure, compounded by the risk of their own removal. Additionally, there could be the lack of a good alternative, or fear of disruption in personal relationships. Whatever the reason, this can be a serious problem in organisations, and lead to real difficulties in understanding them and the behaviours being exhibited.

The dramatic impact CEO's or senior management can have on companies is illustrated in the cases above. Two major international companies failed in Australia within two years as a direct result of the leadership.

To summarise, managing is more about execution, organisation and control, with a focus on tasks, processes and efficiency of operations. This is done by setting goals, timelines, performance indicators, feedback controls and delegation of authority. Leading, on the other hand is about vision and inspiration, respect and trust. It's about influencing people to behave in a way because they want to, rather than having to!

Having looked at some personal examples of dysfunctional leaders or leadership and associated cultures, let's have a look at two well-known American companies where the leadership and culture are widely admired.

Southwest airlines are famous for their fun-loving service-centric culture fostered by Herb Kelleher, a billionaire and lawyer who co-founded the company in the 1970's. He emphasised employees being the heart of the company and his commitment to putting employees first created a highly engaged, playful, dynamic and achievement-oriented workforce. Just reading about them made me wish I'd had the opportunity to work with them.

Hubspot is a very successful American software company founded in 2006. Its founders Brian Halligan and Dharmesh Shah emphasised transparency, autonomy, and a commitment to work life balance. They championed flexible working relationships, a results-oriented environment and open communications to encourage employee success.

In both these cases we see similar traits in the leaders and leadership that put employees first or central to their operations. This focus encourages employee loyalty and commitment, risk taking and innovation, achievement orientation and high standards of work.

Great organisations and cultures such as these do not happen overnight. They require long term commitment and nurturing with consistent leadership and maintenance of the values inherent in such cultures. A change of leadership can cause dramatic changes as in the examples we looked at.

The Crew, like family?

From birth we learn to live in our special spacecraft or organisation known as our family. It is in this special organisation, that without realising it or understanding it, but inevitably and subconsciously, we first learn about leaders, structure, culture, decision making, communication, interpersonal relationships, goals, motivation and competition. We also learn about emotions and feelings such as love, hate, trust and respect. We carry this learning into our later life whether consciously or unconsciously. For example, research has shown that many successful entrepreneurs lost parents early in life. Young children do not understand death and thus death can be seen as desertion. This then results in them, as adults, to a loss of trust in others, and only trust in oneself. This does not only lead to an entrepreneurial or a self-reliant work focus, but also to frequently having difficulty in maintaining any deep personal relationships as they cannot give their trust to others. They subconsciously fear the same desertion and let down they experienced when they trusted a parent. It can also make them very difficult to live with in work and family settings.

Unless we inherit, build our own organisation, or become a chief executive and dictate structure and culture, most of us will spend our time as lower-level crew. Whether we realise it or not, and mostly, as with the family we do not, we confront all the similar issues we have faced or learned in our family. It is this learning that will tend to dictate how we behave and relate to others in organisations we enter. The organisations of course will attempt to shape us to fit their culture, or what they think is their culture. Thus, almost inevitably, we will experience either a cultural fit or clash, though not normally recognising it as such. Let us explore some personal examples that integrate leaders, teams, cultures and individual behaviour!

My First Commercial Employment and Life-Changing Lesson

After the Fleet Air Arm injury the Australian Navy offered me a pension or an operation. At the age of 19, I took the operation and the three months' recuperation. I was then discharged to a Sydney where I knew no one and had absolutely no idea what I could do for work. I first found accommodation at Stratford Manor. It was a property owned by the previous German Ambassador to Australia. We got on famously and he helped me scour newspapers for employment opportunities. One had an advertisement for an Executive Trainee with Gillette. I rang them and was asked to attend an interview. I did so and, wonderfully, the next day I was offered the job.

I accepted and the following day arrived to start work. I was met by Fred Webster, the managing director and a fantastic mentor. I called him "Sir," as I would have in the navy.

He said, I have never been knighted David. I am Mr Webster in the office and everywhere else I'm Fred. This is the first example of the culture and norms that Fred Webster established for his organisation.

He told me I was their first executive trainee, and I'd start on the factory shop floor, taking stock of our inventory of razors and our cosmetic products. From there I would go through each department before I'd become a member of the sales team. On the factory floor we checked inventory twice each day, down to one razor blade and one bottle top in cosmetics. What precision! I was then progressed through the other departments such as accounts and brand marketing until I knew every system. The systems were amazing. Every territory had its client book. Suburban ones were S Books and country ones were C books. Each client had a record card, and the call route was the most time-efficient possible. Records were made of every call; a daily report on sales and merchandising was written and posted every afternoon to Head Office, in pre-addressed priority mail fabric envelopes. This was Australia-wide and each Friday there was a sales meeting. The national statistics for the previous week were displayed in graph form, showing how every sales territory and individual compared nationally. This was phenomenal in that snail mail era, as was the culture of achievement, comradeship and team spirit developed and constantly reinforced by Fred Webster. As in other companies the overarching culture is largely dictated by the chief executive and their behaviours. In no other company I have known were sales staff given the status they were in Gillette, at the top of the pyramid. Fred Webster emphasised to everyone that without sales no one had a job.

Gillette was the most efficient and effective company I have ever encountered, bar none. I discovered later that for many years it was among the most profitable companies in America. Soon, I was out as an executive salesman, following the way I'd been taught using professional sales visuals. I was as nervous as a kitten, stressed and felt self-conscious and awkward, but I followed the sales rule book as I had been taught.

Our razor territories were also cosmetic territories, but the two were covered by different representatives, so each could give feedback on the other. I was astounded when, at a Friday meeting, Peter, an experienced rep told me clients were complaining about the new high-pressure salesman: me. I had to do something about this. I did and learned a life-changing lesson with a life-changing outcome.

Life-changing lessons. Do not be afraid to be honest nor be afraid to ask for help.

I went back to every single account on my four territories. There were two suburban razor and cosmetics and two country territories. In every case, I apologised, and explained I had come from the Navy, had never been a salesman, had only done what I'd been taught to do, and had been uncomfortable doing it. I said I would like the chance to do things differently, would appreciate their help and guidance, and I'd honour their trust. The outcome was remarkable, as I said above. The shop owners gave me unfettered access to their stores and stock. I would walk into a friendly greeting, check stock levels, order stock including any new lines, erect some sales material, get a signature and, with a "see you next time, Phil," go to my next call.

It was taking such a brief time to make calls that I could finish every day by 11am. So, I would make initiative calls to open new accounts, then, as many of my territories had beaches, I would go surfing. Three months later, at a Friday meeting, I learned I was the top sales representative in Australia in all assessment! This led to another problem. I was taken aside on a Friday night by the other representatives. They told me that if I wanted to stay part of the team, and not be shunned and put in Coventry, I had got to drop my game; they felt I was making them all look incompetent, particularly being the youngest by quite a few years.

This was my introduction to group membership requiring my compliance to group norms. This is taken to extremes in outlaw motorcycle gangs, other criminal groups, some religious groups and cults. I readily complied as team members engaged in social activities almost every weekend, and they were my social life. On reflection not unlike motorcycle gangs. I remained the top performer but did a lot more surfing. I am sure Fred Webster had seen this as he often commented on my healthy tan. He then told me he would be transferring me to Victoria, another state, as State Manager Elect as the current manager was resigning. At age 20 I had neither the confidence nor faith in myself to handle the responsibility in this role. I did transfer to Melbourne and had a very wild twenty first birthday there, but despite Fred Webster's seeking to dissuade me, and with real regret I resigned from Gillette, and sailed to England on the infamous Fairsky cruise ship. While I did not recognise it at the time, I'd been given my first real lessons in understanding organisational structure, systems, leadership, culture, management, group dynamics and interpersonal relationships.

Culture clash and other important lessons

Arriving in England, as did most young people, I took on a variety of jobs to pay for travel through UK and Europe. They ranged from clerical to pick and shovel work, but the standout was as an account executive with the W.H.Smith subsidiary Alacra, an office systems company headquartered in London. In applying, I experienced my one and only group selection process. Some forty applicants for five positions were in the same room waiting to be interviewed. It was a pretty daunting experience! Over 50% of applicants, after looking around the room, elected not to be interviewed and left, especially when post interview some applicants rushed out almost crying. When it came my turn, the managing director Dicky Dyke handed me a glass ashtray and said "I'm the purchasing officer for British Rail. Tell me why I should buy these ashtrays". I said that they were low cost, virtually indestructible and functionally well designed. I got no further, was thanked and asked to wait outside. Subsequently, I was a successful applicant, and met the other four. It turned out we were all ex-military. Four ex-army officers and me ex-navy so we had a natural bond, though I was the youngest by some ten years.

The outcome was the selection of five ex-military candidates familiar with military processes. This outcome was also dangerous. You had five ex-military people who immediately formed a cohesive team built around their shared norms and values and not those of Alacra. Cohesive teams with positive leadership can achieve amazing things. Conversely if negatively led they can be a powerfully obstructive or dissident group. This proved to be the case with Alacra.

Understanding why is important. Many companies pursue and promote the development of strong teams without realising they are potentially forging a double-edged sword. They need to recognise it is essential to complement team building with good leading and leaders. If they don't, they will lose staff, nearly always the best ones first who are easily employable elsewhere.

I was hauled over the coals when I first arrived at our London office, wearing a smart grey suit, pale green shirt, green tie and brown suede shoes. The sales manager, an accountant, told me to go home and return with a black suit, black shoes, white shirt and a subtle tie! Luckily, I was able to do so. We then all commenced a rigorous training program in office systems such as purchasing, sales, payroll, inventory etc. Our job was to analyse a company's existing systems, and design new ones utilising Alacra's proprietary multiple page stationery.

Out in the field I achieved reasonable but not particularly special results. So, surprisingly, I was asked to see what I could do with a major engineering company. One with massive potential where previous staff had failed. I went to the company having got an interview with the managing director. I was ushered into his quarter acre office where he was sitting behind a massive desk. I introduced myself and he went Ahem! Colonial, are you? I couldn't help myself and replied "No! I'm a pommie bastard like you actually!" Huh! He said a damned Aussie! Do you know Keith Miller? What a great cricketer and larrikin Nugget was. I played against him with The Gentlemen at Lord's". I said I knew of him only and Geoffrey, we were now on first name terms, said we'll talk over lunch. We did and as a result he said. See what you can do young man. I'll be interested to look at your results. After 3 weeks work, I took my results to him showing major efficiency and cost savings through optimising work flows and integrating systems. He liked what he saw and gave me the go ahead. I took the order back to our office. The sales manager was stunned. It was going to be, by a significant margin, the largest single order the company had ever had. He asked me how I'd achieved this. I told him the story and he sacked me on the spot, berating me publicly about my loutish behaviour, and telling me that was not how we spoke to or treated our clients. I was clearing my desk when a raging Dicky Dyke arrived and told me to stop. He then stormed into the sales managers office, slammed the door and a major altercation took place, with Dicky telling the manager, including a few expletives, it was the end that mattered and not the means. Everyone heard it. Not surprising, as Dicky Dyke had worked his way from the shop floor to Managing Director, having previously been the youngest warrant officer in the British Army. Both remarkable feats.

None of us five had any respect for the accountant sales manager and rejected him as our leader. As a result, we decided that when we all had alternative jobs we would resign together, and we did on the same day.

We celebrated by going to a famous Indian restaurant in Piccadilly. It was packed and we were not getting served. Suddenly Ivor, who had been a colonel in the Indian Army, roared out something and next minute we were surrounded by smiling and laughing Indian waiters. We asked Ivan what he had said? He said he had roared in Urdu "get over here you lazy buggers or I'll be eating your balls for breakfast"! We had wonderful service, great food and a great time to the envy of other diners!

There is an important lesson in Ivor's roared command to the Indian waiters. It could have been received as rude, offensive and arrogant. It clearly was not, judging by the smiles and laughter. This illustrates the importance of context, content, manner and tone in conveying totally different messages with the same words. I realised this when first arriving in Australia. The term "pommie bastard" could be a term of endearment or derision, diametrically opposite messages depending on context, manner and tone. I experienced both! So be aware!

Another story about Ivan. The power of presence and perceived authority. One lunchtime we five. In our dark suits, went for a walk in Oxford Street and into Selfridges, the famous department store. Ivan went to the salesperson in the men's shoe department, and said he wanted the displays reorganised. Right now and how! Without questioning Ivor, the staff member started doing it. Ivor repeated this in three more menswear sections, leaving a trail of hyperactivity and some confusion behind us as we left the store.

This behavioural response to unquestioned authority is well known. Probably the most well-known research in the 1960's was Stanley Milgram's Obedience Experiment where participants inflicted almost lethal electric shocks to a victim. Thirty-nine Psychiatrists had estimated that only one person in one thousand would give the maximum 450-volt charge. However, in the experiment 62% of participants did so, to the disbelief and shock of the psychiatrists. The research became known as the Auschwitz Experiment as it was designed to explain some of the inmate behaviours in Nazi concentration camps. I have emulated Ivor's authoritative approach quite a number of times in different situations with similar behavioural outcomes, so Milgram's research is still valid after sixty years.

There are other interesting lessons here. In the group selection process, we can see that self-perception and self-doubt, purely based on the physical appearance of others, made people forego an interview by leaving, despite the fact they may have had the skills and knowledge required or valued. It also illustrates, as with Ivor, the power of presence, dress and first impressions. In groups in organisations there is a similar problem with self-censorship in the presence of authority figures. This often results from a group culture fearful of offending those members with senior status, thus inhibiting open or contentious views and risk taking, and severely limiting a group's potential.

Academic Groups and Leadership

In writing this, I'm reminded of doing Economics 200 in my first degree. We were all in the lecture theatre when a rather portly, casually dressed lecturer in a Harris Tweed jacket with patched elbows and underpants exposed above his corduroy trousers, appeared in front of us. Indeed, he was the epitome of an Oxford don.

"My name," he said with a slight lisp, "is Walter Elltith [Elltiss] and I'm your lecturer for this semester. I must start by saying that I hope you haven't purchased the course textbook. If you have, dispose of it for the best price you can get. We will not be using it. I read it on the flight from England and frankly it is rubbish. The man clearly does not understand what he is talking about! Wow! What an opening gambit. He immediately had 110% attention from 300 students. Walter went on to say he expected us to read broadly, and he would suggest texts and journals relevant to what we were discussing.

That semester was my best experience at university. Walter made economics come alive with great stories in the fields of agriculture, manufacturing, and government among others, as well as the role of invention and innovation. The lecture hall was always packed with students eagerly anticipating the new stories. At the end of the semester, Walter advised us that after suggesting the economics department might be somewhat neophobic or staffed by Luddites, both correct, he would be returning to Oxford. I know I can speak on behalf of every student in that class in saying he was probably the best lecturer we had ever encountered.

On finishing his last lecture, Walter was accorded the only non-stop standing ovation I have ever seen, outside of stage performances, until he bowed, waved goodbye and exited the theatre. I can add that exam results were excellent and a tribute to his leadership. To relate this to understanding organisations, our student group was effectively an organisational group with a common goal: to pass the examination for Economics 200. What we experienced was a group that unexpectedly had a great leader. He was a leader who was there for us, a leader from whom we could learn, a leader who we could trust and respect, and a leader who had leadership conferred upon him by those excited to be led by him. This is true leadership and the antithesis of leadership acquired through the assumption of a role or a structural change where generally both are based on some arcane authority structure.

My Rock Star Moment and another Important Lesson

Don't be afraid to follow gut feelings or to blindside your audience.

I had not long joined academia and was a lowly tutor. I'd done a lot of pro bono work with Rotary, conducting training workshops for over 10,000 participants, and for many hundreds of small business owners throughout Western Australia. Rotary then asked me if I would give a presentation on marketing in an important seminar-workshop with some 300 attendees at a major hotel. The three morning speakers were to be the premier, Sir Charles Court, Professor Roy Lourens, head of UWA Business School, and the CEO of the Confederation of Industry. I was the first post-lunch speaker, the worst time slot. I had made copious notes and summarised them onto cards, but I was not happy with my planned presentation. I thought it was, despite the work put into it, humdrum, conventional, ordinary and uninspiring.

During the presentations of all the illustrious morning speakers, I had taken notes on what they were saying. On the spur of the moment, I decided to throw caution to the wind and threw away all my notes. I stood up in front of my 300 attendees, many of whom wanted to have a nap after lunch and said "Well, you have listened to all the speakers this morning and now I'm going to tell you why they were all wrong". Suddenly I had everyone's attention! I spoke quite passionately about needing to know what our real markets were and what we were really selling, whether a product or a service. I cited Charles Revson, a cofounder of Revlon, the cosmetics company. When asked what Revlon sold, his answer was, "We sell hope!" They sold hope to women seeking to make themselves more attractive or beautiful. This then dictated their marketing, showing images of women with looks or poise you could aspire to through using Revlon products. I then talked about Qantas. It was not in the transport industry. It was competing for discretionary holiday travel, tourism and adventure dollars. We then looked at other industries with the same question. What are you really selling? Is your marketing targeting the right market or the right motives?

I didn't use a single note and spoke to the audience, not at them. On finishing I was blown away. I got a standing ovation and people rushed up to me to say that it was the most inspirational presentation they had ever attended. I also got several companies offering consulting assignments. The important lesson from this was that it is best to speak from the heart, speak with emotion and engage with your audience. It proved to be a one-off. I never had an experience quite like that again, but the lesson paid dividends in every subsequent career.

Understanding Projection, Confronting It and More

Psychological projection is a defence mechanism where individuals attribute their own unwanted or unacceptable thoughts, emotions, or characteristics to another person. This can result in the projection of positive traits as well, but it commonly involves projecting negative aspects of oneself onto others, allowing you to avoid recognising and confronting your own feelings or behaviours.

Once, when I was attending a Tavistock Group Exploratory Conference at Stratford-upon-Avon in England, there was one group member who was really annoying me with his comments and what I saw as a know-it-all attitude. One objective of the Conference was to achieve self-learning, so I thought, what the hell, and walked over to this team member and asked, "Do you think I'm a complete wanker"?

He said "Yes, how did you know that?"

I said, "Because I think you are one as well." It was the start of a friendship that has lasted over 40 years. The secret to this interaction was that I was the one to put myself down and thus expose myself and risk the outcome, whatever it might be. As you can imagine, it would have been a very different outcome had I gone to him and said something like, "You know I'm really fed up with your behaviour and think you are a complete wanker." I am sure he would have become defensive or aggressive and I doubt we would have become the best of friends.

So, if in groups or meetings you get some serious negative vibes about someone, you may well be projecting, and I have suggested a way you could get a great positive outcome. You must take the initial risk, drop your protective defence barriers, and be prepared to face the outcome.

Selecting and Appointing Leaders

At the Tavistock GEC, one of the initial tasks the group had to do was select a leader. This process is something that is important to understand in organisations. It proved an interesting process. We had all these high-powered executives in the group, with some of them clearly wanting to be leader, as they were the leaders in their own companies. But in the group, they faced difficult issues. If they proposed themselves, they would face a high risk of rejection, as they were no different in status to any other member. Also, there were no subgroups or power brokers who could muster the numbers or be influenced to support them, though some attempted this. It was very clear that almost all the male members would have liked to be asked to be leader. At the same time, no one seemed able to find a reason to recommend anyone without causing significant damage to egos. I was a learning observer, as I had been invited by my Tavistock supervisor to attend the conference and could see from all the non-verbal cues all the males were unwilling to vote for any other male as their leader, but we still had to select one.

The solution in the circumstances became an obvious one. We would appoint the one woman in our group as leader. This meant there was no loss of face by any male group member and no damage to any male egos. And so, it was. Our female consulting psychologist became undisputed leader. How many times have we all seen similar scenarios in private and public sector organisations. This is not to infer that female leaders are selected for this reason. Far from it, as there are many fantastic female leaders. It does illustrate that leaders can be selected because they are considered malleable or represent the least threat to others. In Australia, Prime Minister William (Billy) McMahon was considered one such person. However, in most cases we usually have cliques, factions or groups who wheel and deal to reinforce power bases, careers, or other agendas in leader selection processes. There is another issue we need to consider in the appointment of managers and leaders. This is the very common practice of promoting someone based on performance in their current position, rather than the qualities required for the new role. This has probably resulted, more than any other procedure, in the promotion of the wrong persons into managerial or leader roles. A classic example of this is the top salesperson being appointed to a sales or marketing manager role. The roles are totally different, and so are the skills and attributes required. Suddenly you need people, leader and organisational skills, and are reliant on the performance of others for success. These are vastly different skill requirements to those of a self-reliant and beat-your-colleagues salesperson. Similarly, people who have shown good administrative skills get appointed to leader roles. These examples are both closely linked to the Peter Principle, where people are promoted to a level where they are no longer competent. It suggests, with considerable supporting evidence, that there are many people in roles where they are not competent, for all kinds of reasons. This is very common at the supervisory level, where like salespeople, good tradespersons or shop floor people are promoted to supervisor roles requiring a very different skill set, without having had the training.

This had been recognised by industry and led to a major Federal Government national project. This was to develop management competencies for Australia. It was called the NGMS project, National Generic Management Skills, and I was appointed to head up the project. We held meetings in every state and territory with all stakeholders, business owners, managers, unions and government. I got T-shirts made for all our team members. These were in two colours. Green for core team members and grey for affiliates, with a large black duck like Daffy Duck logo giving everyone the finger, with NGMS under him. These were mandatory for team meetings, and apart from helping create a great cohesive team, led to one serious and one fun outcome. The serious one was that I was threatened by Warner Brothers, the trademark owners of Daffy Duck with being sued for breaching their copyright. This was settled amicably, when I showed invoices for getting the artwork done and saying that nothing was being sold. The second was when asked by a lady at one of our meeting places in north Queensland what NGMS stood for, I said, on the spur of the moment "Never Get Much Sex" to which she replied I know that problem!

Once the management competencies were established, requiring a twelve-month time frame, they formed the foundation of a new national Diploma in Frontline Management, for which our team and other subject specialists, wrote the learning materials. Most companies across Australia then used this as their primary training tool for supervisors or newly appointed managers.

I should explain my Daffy giving the finger! This was me saying that this project was going to be run differently. My team were first and central! Instead of the government bureaucracy doing it, I managed the whole project. This included agendas, hotel accommodation, air travel, sometimes upgrades to business class, plus all meals and entertainment. We stayed at five-star hotels, ate at five-star restaurants, sometimes taken by limousines, with cocktails or mocktails prior to dinner. We went horse riding, played tennis, and even had a flight to a tourist island, courtesy of a friend who owned the aircraft. This was all done well within the project budget that was based on three-star hotel accommodation and similar restaurants. I had advised the team members on day one that I'd do this. In return I had said that I expected no one to play the usual games with their per diem allowances. These included staying with friends, or buying a pie for lunch, while billing for hotel stays and restaurant meals. In short, we were going to practice what we were preaching. The project of over twelve months was great fun, enjoyed by all with almost one hundred percent attendance. The project was completed on time, under budget and to a high standard. It illustrates one belief that I've always held. It is that fun and enjoyment at work are totally compatible with efficiency and effectiveness, and a highly desirable feature of any organisational culture. With the success of this project, I was given another one to lead and manage on senior management competencies. However, it was on condition I did not repeat the perceived extravagances of the previous project, even though they were all below budget. This was because it had created precedents that made the conventional systems look incompetent, clunky and costly. Nonetheless, it is clearly illustrative of the inefficiencies and costs inherent in most bureaucracies, where efficiencies become subordinate to unchallenged processes.

Miscellanea in Understanding Organisations

Getting Untainted Conversations

An interesting experiment in getting a different perspective on groups and group meetings is to simply get under the table at a group meeting, and just listen to the conversations taking place. We did this at the Tavistock Group Exploratory Conference. It eliminates the clutter and white noise associated with all the visual cues and interactions taking place. Now isolated from this, you hear all the nuances of conversations from different tones, emphasis, pauses, interjections etc. It presents quite a different picture of what is taking place. This is a purer picture as it is simply the real conversations, which potentially tell a quite different story. You should explain your rationale before doing this or you may be referred to the company shrink. It could be less dramatic, simpler, and less risky to sit behind a screen!

Casting the Organisation as a Drama

A technique or process you could find useful, in getting to better understand organisational behaviour in different situations, is to bestow key individuals with different roles, as though the organisation was a stage drama. Shakespearean ones are good to use! I have found this can delightfully explain the actual or real roles and relationships in an organisation as opposed to those supposed to exist.

For example, through this lens, you can see someone whose role is that of king or queen, frequently not the persons the organisation has in those roles. Others could be the king maker, chief advisor, the court jester, the judge, the executioner, the assassin, the brown-nose, the treasurer or the prince or princess, who are the aspirants to become king or queen.

Suddenly you are amidst a drama that has come alive, and you have a whole new basis for understanding what is happening around you with potential explanations of people's behaviours. Of course, if you are a member of the organisation this becomes more complex as you are part of the dynamic. You may need to seek clarity on your own perceived role from an honest friend and or ask them to nominate who they believe should have the roles that you bestowed on others. This can be an enlightening activity leading to a real and different understanding.

Objectivity

How many times have we heard people say that they are looking at things objectively? In the same light how often do we say, "Looking at it objectively…"? Moreover, how many times have we been in groups and been told, "We really must look at this objectively" We are talking about the impossible! We are human beings. We cannot possibly be objective about anything. I repeat, we cannot be objective about anything. Everything that we say or do or think about is inevitably subjective and there is nothing we can do that will change that. We are a product of our past and everything that our brain has absorbed. This has a lifelong impact on everything we believe, think, see, or do. Being objective is a fallacy. We are not computers. At least not yet!

Management Textbooks

I do not think I'd get too much disagreement in saying that, with few exceptions, management textbooks are among the driest, most boring and stultifying books ever written, with the propensity to turn students off the subject rather than enthusing them. When teaching postgrad management, I never had a course textbook. How could any author hope to address, in one text, the vast array and richness of work done by social psychologists, psychiatrists, ethologists, anthropologists, sociologists, or organisational theorists such as Jung, Freud, Fromm, Mead, Lewin, McGregor, Von Bertalanffy, Herzberg, Maslow, Weber, Drucker, or Schein, to name just a few authors.

Mostly the texts are simply repackaged, and re-engineered contributions from the above and others, written in styles that depersonalise everything. The texts simply do not come to life. As I said to my students, "I don't want a text regurgitated like a bird feeding its young."

You are here to learn, so let us do it collectively and do some research". One of the books on management that I thoroughly enjoyed was the book *Up the Organization: How to Stop the Corporation from Stifling People and Strangling Profits.* It was written by Robert C. Townsend. This book, published in 1970, describes unconventional and humorous insights into corporate management and leadership practices. In it, Robert Townsend, a former CEO of Avis, who is often attributed with turning Avis into America's second largest car rental company, shares his thoughts and ideas on how organisations can be more effective, innovative, and employee friendly. His thoughts and ideas were radical at the time and appealed to me immensely. If you have not read it, please do, as it's still radical, relevant and really entertaining.

Townsend, however, was in a unique position to implement his program. He was the CEO, and he had the backing of his board. It is rare for anyone to be in such a position where they can unilaterally reshape an entire company in every aspect of its operations: structurally, culturally and functionally. Digressing slightly, you can look at history books in a similar light to management texts. Different authors can write about the same period in history with one being a rousing, page-turning fascinating adventure story while the other is as dry as dust. I hope that the journey I'm now taking you on will be more like the former.

Two Perspectives on Organisational Behaviour

Most, in fact all the textbooks that I have read on organisational behaviour focus on behaviours within the organisation or environment. These variously focus on structure, culture, individuals, groups, teams, interactions, communication, decision processes and so on. This is all great stuff, but there is a totally different perspective you can take. This is to take a macro view and look at the organisation as a living entity and look at its behaviour in the same way as though it was an individual. When this is done it can become quite evident that organisations can and do exhibit similar behavioural traits as individuals. These can be positive, enhancing development. However, equally, and not infrequently, they can prove pathological, self-destructive, or even potentially suicidal. We have looked at some examples. I have seen little literature that looks at organisations through this lens. That is, as though they were individuals with individual behavioural characteristics, with behaviour susceptible to analysis or psychoanalysis as a living entity. I hope there are some as it would be a rich field for research.

The only text I read in the late 1980s that got close to looking at organisations from this perspective, though focussed on groups, was called *Microcosm* by Philip E Slater. As far as I am aware it is a very difficult book to find. My copy is long lost. The last price I saw was $530 for a copy from Amazon. However, here is an overview. If you can find the original, prepare for a fascinating and challenging read.

Microcosm: Structural, Psychological, and Religious Evolution in Groups by Philip E. Slater, a sociologist was published in 1966. It explores the dynamics of groups, societies, and human behaviour through a multidisciplinary lens. Here are the key issues addressed in the book:

Interdisciplinary Approach: Slater takes an interdisciplinary approach to understanding group behaviour, drawing on sociology, psychology, anthropology, and religious studies. He combines insights from various fields to explore the complex dynamics of human groups. In this way Slater's work relates well to General Systems Theory.

Structural Analysis: Here he delves into the structural aspects of groups, examining how patterns of authority, hierarchy, and power influence group behaviour and individuals' roles within groups.

Psychological Insights: Slater explores the psychological dimensions of group behaviour, including the ways that individuals' needs for identity, security, and belonging can shape their interactions within groups. This is not dissimilar to the work done by Wilfred Bion on dependency, flight-fight and pairing, that we explore later.

Religious and Mythological Elements: He delves into the religious and mythological aspects of group life. He discusses the way shared beliefs and rituals can contribute to group cohesion and identity but can also lead to conflict. This is seen in major religions and sects or branches within those religions. Examples are the Sunni and Shia branches of Islam, where many of each do not accept members of the other branch as fellow Muslims. Christianity has had similar issues with Catholics and Protestants.

Evolutionary Perspective: Slater uses an evolutionary perspective to examine the development and transformation of groups over time. He explores the ways groups adapt and change in response to both internal and external pressures. This is evident in religions, governments, work organisations and other societal groups. This again has strong links to General Systems Theory that was emerging at the same time as Slater's research.

Critique of Modern Society: Microcosm offers a critical analysis of modern society and its impact on individuals and groups. Slater discusses the way societal structures and norms can influence group dynamics and individual behaviour. We can see this in the authoritarian countries such as China, Russia, Afghanistan, Syria, North Korea, and Vietnam and moves to displace democratic or sectarian societies in countries like

Venezuela, Turkiye and Poland. It is also evident in the recognition of groups, especially those of young people seeking more action to mitigate the effects of climate change.

In its day, Microcosm earned much attention, in both academic and non-academic circles, for its innovative approach to understanding group behaviour. It contributed substantial original research to discussions about group dynamics, social psychology, and cultural studies that is still valid.

It really was a truly notable work in the field of sociology and group dynamics. It offered a unique perspective on the ways in which individuals and groups interact, adapt, and evolve within the complex fabric of society. Most of the specific references in the book are rooted in the cultural and social context of the 1960s, when it was written. However, its broader insights into group behaviour continue to be highly relevant for understanding human societies and organisations more than 60 years later.

There is so much remarkable research in this text, it's hard to provide more than the brief oversight above. It is highly powerful and particularly relevant to the many and varied contemporary militia, conspiracy theorist, racist, religious and myriad other extremist groups and cults. It looks at the subtle, yet destructive and dehumanising ways that groups exert power and seek total control over followers or adherents. This is done to obtain absolute compliance and submission to the norms and to the lawmakers in the cult. It of course also happens in organisations. In many parts it is decidedly dark and almost frightening, especially when Slater discusses punishments meted out within the groups, including acts of ritual murder of nonconforming members, and even group leaders, that are carried out by the group.

Investigations into Scientology, Hillsong, the Moonies, outlaw motorcycle gangs, and similar organisations, illustrate and reinforce what Slater described and explained some 60 years ago. So, little has changed, and many people worldwide are still getting socially and mentally damaged by these groups. Such groups are also leading to disruptive change at the societal and national level in many countries. The invasion of the White House in America in 2021 starkly illustrates this, as does the rise and influence of nazi and similar right-wing groups in other countries. What we are witnessing are increasingly disturbing examples of cultural evolution or change.

Qantas and Cultural Death by a Thousand Cuts

I've never looked at Qantas professionally as an analyst, but I've had a long association with it, and feel a great sadness at how it's been treated and what it has become. I first flew with Qantas from Sydney to Heathrow in London in 1958. It was in a Super Constellation of which I still have photos. It took three days, and the cost of the one-way flight was my annual navy salary. Later in life the first time I entered a Qantas business lounge, courtesy of my Gold Card, I was reprimanded by a lounge staff member for wearing jeans! How things have changed.

In the early days and prior to privatisation, Qantas was the envy of the aviation industry, with many airlines, including the widely admired Singapore Airlines, trying to emulate it. From my subjective and biased point of view, the key factor that made Qantas such a great airline was its culture and its staff, particularly the staff in the aircraft. They were efficient and effective but at the same time there was lots of humour, fun and laughter. The staff always seemed to be really enjoying themselves and this feeling was conveyed to passengers.

It was a wonderful culture and an absolute pleasure to travel. Also, there seemed to be an element of freedom and autonomy in the crew's actions that seems totally lacking today. For example, on a flight to San Francisco I just mentioned to the steward that it was the birthday of the young lady next to me. The steward disappeared and then reappeared with a bottle of champagne. With a big smile, he said, "You can now enjoy a champagne breakfast on us." I can recall similar events over the years but not in recent decades.

To me, it is fairly evident that the dramatic culture change, and death by a thousand cuts commenced when James Strong took over as CEO of Qantas. He purchased and merged Australian Airlines, of which he had been CEO, with Qantas and then proceeded to float Qantas as a public company in 1995. There is no doubt that he did great things operationally for Qantas. He did this with the acquisition of other airlines, purchase of new, more efficient aircraft, along with a strong focus on safety and customer amenities and service. Qantas profits reached new highs under his leadership. However, friends of mine who had been long term employees of Qantas said that this period was when the great culture that made Qantas unique was suppressed and progressively undermined, with the emphasis now simply on efficiency and profits. I need to add that management were now awarding themselves very generous salary and performance packages.

As with many poorly designed motivation or performance incentives, such as those in Qantas, you end up with goal displacement and behaviours focused on the short term at the expense of the long term.

This happens at all levels and departments in organisations, and the law of unintended consequences frequently prevails. With sales incentives staff can oversell, get bonuses and leave the aftermath to the next salesperson. In the area of safety, where meeting safety targets leads to big bonuses, you get under or non-reporting of safety breaches or worker injuries that would result in non-receipt of bonuses. The worst corporate outcomes, however, are those that occur when senior management goals of long-term growth and profitability of the company are replaced. Maximising personal income and profits at the expense of long-term organisational goals become drivers, but eventually someone must pay the piper. Those paying the piper can be incoming management, shareholders, corporate image or brand value and most likely all of them.

With James Strong's departure, Geoff Dixon was CEO for a relatively stable and uneventful seven years, but then Alan Joyce became CEO, and this was seen by many as the death knell for the Australian aviation icon, beloved by many Australians. Under his management approach, and later backed by his Chairman, the Qantas objective clearly seemed to be profit at any cost, by using any means, whether legal, illegal, immoral, unconscionable, dishonest or destructive. Indeed, some of the actions taken under Joyce were like those seen in paranoid and tyrannical authoritarian regimes.

I humorously suggested to a friend that I wondered when Joyce would, like Putin, call on the Wagner group to implement his policies. If Qantas was a patient in a psychiatric facility, it would take a very good multidisciplinary team to work out how it could first be brought back from a near death experience, and secondly how it could be rehabilitated and brought back to its former role as the True Spirit of Australia, trusted by employees, unions and the Australian public.

I'm a rare lifetime Qantas club member and, in recent years have always travelled business class. Qantas business class standards have been in constant decline, particularly on interstate routes. On recent flights I've declined all the business class meal offerings, a choice of two, asking if I could just have cheese and biscuits, to be told they didn't have any. I was then given a choice of either one red or one white wine, no spirits and limited juices. However, the greatest failure on the same trip was when my partner, who had requested a vegetarian meal, was told they had run out, and this is hard to believe, she was offered an apple! I reiterate that this was Qantas business class! I can only imagine that, based on this, the economy class passengers would have been lucky to get a bag of pretzels. It's difficult to believe that this was once one of the world's premier airlines, one that I was proud of and where possible, always travelled on. Hopefully, under new leadership it will see renewal, with a focus on profits through service and quality, but it will not be easy.

If Qantas was not in such a dominant and protected position within the Australian aviation market, such major cultural and operational changes could have proved fatal. Qantas is a great illustration of how the culture of an organization can be changed dramatically by its leader, and leadership team. It also illustrates how this can result in major long-term damage, while those responsible escape and enjoy their ill-gotten golden parachutes. Alan Joyce's was from memory twenty-four million dollars.

Groups and Organisations

As indicated earlier when looking at Slater's research, the study of groups and group dynamics is one of the most interesting, fascinating and rewarding fields of knowledge in understanding organisations. Groups are the fundamental building blocks of any organisation. They come in all sizes and shapes and are structured in a multitude of ways. There can be horizontal groups, vertical groups or multidimensional or matrix groups. The organisation is typically a matrix of groups, increasing in complexity with size or geographical dispersion. The one thing that one can expect with a fair degree of certainty is that, if you manage to identify, plot, or chart the actual groups in an organisation, it is unlikely to be much like the formal structure beloved by structural theorists, and as portrayed in management texts. The actual structure and relationship of groups is quite amorphous and dynamic. They constantly change as they and the organisation respond to changes in their environments.

Senior management is frequently unaware of this, as it tends to occur at the group level. In fact, if organisations waited for senior management to tell them how and when to change to meet changed conditions, the company would probably fail. Marketing groups will change to meet changed market conditions, and finance departments to meet changed regulatory environments. Rarely will the different departments be aware of all the changes taking place in other departments. This is despite changes in one almost inevitably influencing other departments or divisions in some way, and often being the cause of significant interdepartmental or intergroup conflict.

Once, when a manager in a company while studying for my first degree, I sensed this problem, as issues were often cropping up between sales, warehousing and finance. I called an open meeting and invited staff from all divisions to attend. Each division then explained the problems created for them by the other divisions. It turned out that each division had no idea of how they were affecting the others. The recognition and understanding of this led to a whole new level of cooperation in resolving the issues. In addition, the resultant strong interdepartmental connections and communication minimised similar future issues.

Not only did such a simple move improve organisational efficiency, but it also promoted a new culture of cooperation rather than conflict. A great result. To further reinforce a point, senior management were not advised, and had no idea this meeting had ever been held. However, no doubt they congratulated themselves on the inexplicable performance improvements!

General Systems Theory

This is something we absolutely must discuss. I was introduced to General Systems Theory (GST) in the late 1970s. It is an inter-disciplinary framework for understanding and analysing complex systems. It originated in the mid-20th century and was first developed by biologist Ludwig von Bertalanffy. I was literally blown away. Suddenly there was this beautiful and elegant theory or theories, not just for one thing but for everything. In reading the work of von Bertalanffy (1901-1972), I realised just how powerful and all-embracing it was, and how it confirmed that I had no real understanding of organisations at all. I think I would go so far as saying that one could never claim to under-stand organisations or indeed organisms or going even fur-ther anything in the natural world of any kind, without having examined or analysed them through the General Systems lens. You may well have done this but without realising you were employing systems thinking.

GST proposes that systems, whether they are biological, social, or mechanical, share common principles and can be studied using a unified approach. Von Bertalanffy argued that the tra-ditional reductionist approach, which focused on analysing systems by breaking them down into their constituent parts, was insufficient for understanding complex systems, espe-cially those in biology, ecology, and social sciences. I recall once hearing a comment about increasing specialisation in every field. It was that if we keep increasing this rate of spe-cialisation, we will end up with people who know everything about nothing. This is less erudite than Von Bertalanffy, but it reinforces his point.

Key principles of General Systems Theory include:

Holism: GST emphasises studying systems holistically, rather than breaking them down into isolated components. It recognises that the interactions among the components are crucial for understanding the system's behaviour as a whole entity. Holistic medicine and health approaches see the body in the same way. If you stop and think about it it's pretty obvious, but we rarely think about it! If a neurosurgeon knew everything about the brain, but knew nothing about the circulatory, endocrine, neural, respiratory, reproductive, or other systems, his knowledge would have extremely limited value. We know that we need to understand how all these systems work together, interact with, and influence each other. A good example is the recent recognition of the importance of the gut-brain axis. Research has shown that the gut has a surprisingly potent influence on the brain. Along with this is the realisation of the importance of gut microbiota in influencing these interactions. Our gut microbiota is dictated by our diet and so our diet can influence our brain. To understand organisations and organisational behaviour you need to look at them in an analogous way. That is, understand the components and the processes but importantly understand how they interact with and mutually influence one another. This is where systems thinking can provide both an understanding and predictive approach to events that have occurred or could occur.

Interdependence: Systems consist of interconnected and interdependent parts. Changes in one part can have ripple effects throughout the system. An example of this is the way climate change is affecting weather patterns around the world, but it is not just weather patterns. Human health, species survival, migration and social structures are just a few systems also

41

influenced. Organisations are evolving and dying, they are geographically relocating, farming and agricultural practices are under threat. Climate change will undoubtedly prove the greatest challenge to mankind's capacity to adapt to or change its environment, in the new epoch of the Anthropocene. It also presents great opportunities and motivation for innovation and change. Many years ago, I was reading about Herman Kahn. He headed up the Hudson Institute, a leading American think tank, and apparently had the highest known IQ. He purportedly said, around the 1960's, that in his view homo sapiens was likely to become the most unsuccessful species in the history of the planet. I believe at the time he was talking about nuclear armageddon, and the USA/Russia cold war, but his statement could prove prophetic if climate change is not managed.

Interdisciplinarity: GST promotes interdisciplinary collaboration, encouraging scientists from various fields to work together to address complex problems. We now see this widely occurring in most fields of research and study. It is also at the core of the Delphi technique that uses multiple rounds of questions sent to experts in many fields and disciplines. They progressively modify their views based on reading the inputs from the other experts. You end up with the collective and consolidated views of experts from all the different fields, as the basis for making major decisions, particularly those addressing the future and international investments. For example, in nineteen eighty I participated in a Shell International Delphi process. One outcome was a forecast of the Berlin Wall falling within a decade. It took 9 years. Another input factor was the increased purchase of military equipment by governments. This had been shown as being closely linked to future political instability and thus increased investment risk. A vital consideration if you were going to invest billions of dollars.

Hierarchy: Systems can be hierarchical, with subsystems nested within larger systems. This hierarchical structure allows for the examination of systems at multiple levels. The organisational company structure is just one example. Others include us, and our circulatory, nervous, endocrine and many other systems coordinated by the brain. As with the brain, the board of a company will only work effectively if the information, communications and feedback it receives from its internal and external environments are accurate and timely. When they are not accurate and timely the risk of making poor decisions has a high probability.

Feedback: Feedback loops are essential in systems, as they help regulate and maintain stability. Feedback can be positive, reinforcing, or negative unbalancing. This is where we face problems with our environment today, as the feedback loops are progressively failing, largely through our impact on them. This then leads to a lack of required actions to maintain homeostasis. The resultant lack of equilibrium and balance is increasingly evident in our planet, nations, organisations, as well as group and individual behaviour.

Boundaries: Systems have boundaries that define their scope. Understanding the boundaries is important for defining what is included in the system, and what is external to it. There are many boundaries in organisations. Important ones are at the front line e.g., in retail or service industries it is the sales, reception or service staff who manage the boundary with the consumer. You also have boundaries between departments and hierarchical levels. Managing these boundaries well is what contributes to cooperation, good relations, and communications as well as a good and healthy culture. How often is your view of an enterprise or another department coloured by how you are treated in your first phone call or visit.

Equifinality: Systems can achieve the same outcome state through different pathways or different initial conditions or state, just as we can in our careers. This concept highlights the flexibility and adaptability of systems. How often do we see chief executives

43

given opportunities to resign, or fired in extreme cases, with a new CEO appointed to take the organisation on a new pathway. Sometimes the new pathway is worse than the old one leading to a far worse state.

A famous or infamous CEO who illustrates this was Jack Welch aka neutron or chainsaw Jack. He joined GE in 1960 as a junior engineer and was appointed as CEO of General Electric in the USA in 1981. At that time one of the world's largest companies. He engaged in ruthless cost cutting, firing over 100,000 people in mass layoffs and closing factories, while investing in and acquiring rather risky companies in risky business fields. In the short term this worked, profits soared, and Jack got rock star status in the business world as the first celebrity CEO. In the long term however, his approach and investments proved disasters. When Jack Walsh left in 2001 after 20 years at the helm, he got a payout of over $400 million, despite the enormous damage he had done. This damage brought GE to its knees when the GFC hit in 2008. Later in 2021, GE was finally split into three small companies, after at one stage being the most valuable company in the world. This was effectively due to one man, who got a $400 million golden handshake, for destroying a once great company! In addition, and even worse, he negatively affected the world-wide corporate social landscape. Jack's ruthless approach led to a highly undesirable social outcome. He used to get every employee evaluated annually, and the bottom 10% were fired every year. You can imagine how this process would have been corrupted to protect friends, family, and those able to reward you. Other major companies then adopted similar approaches. As a direct result job security became a thing of the past in most of corporate America, and then spread internationally. In addition, many of the jobs lost were then offshored. This practice again was adopted by the corporate world in the United States and other countries. It dramatically illustrates how one man's actions can drastically alter business practices and broad-based business cultures, as well as resulting in massive and undesirable social change. When one looks at Qantas it's clear that Joyce was following Chainsaw Jack's rule book, including offshoring jobs. Like with GE this had great short-term results for shareholders, and staggering returns for Joyce, senior managers and the board. The chairman's annual earnings were some $750,000 plus perks worth up to and exceeding $200,000. In the longer term, as with Chainsaw Jack and GEC the outcome was similar, but not as disastrous. This thanks to the Australian public who bailed out Qantas out during Covid, with a two billion dollars loan that Joyce and his board declined to repay. Qantas board members should have raised major questions about Joyce's actions. If they'd had any real knowledge of business management history, they would have recognised the path down which they were being led, and what lay at the end of that path. Like all shareholders, and they would personally have held many shares, they failed to really question how these profits were being made, and what was the long-term impact. As with Chainsaw Jack they seem only to have focussed on the short-term profits, and their board fees, while the company was following a trajectory not unlike GE but fortunately without making the high-risk corporate investments.

Open and Closed Systems: As shown previously, systems can be categorised as open, interacting with their environment, or closed, isolated from their environment. Open systems exchange, in a two-way process matter, energy, and information with their surroundings. Von Bertalanffy's ideas emphasised that most systems are open to their environments, exchanging matter, energy, and information with the outside world. This concept challenged the previously held notion of closed, isolated systems that could be easily controlled. i.e. controlled despite and without reference to the host environment. The simple way of looking at this is to consider yourself. Throughout your life you have been influenced by your family, work and social environments and you have influenced them. I've so often heard parents say something like "how is it that my or our children are so different despite growing up in the same family"? A simple answer is to look and think in a systems way. If you do this, you will realise that they have not grown up in the same family. The first child creates a system of three members with its unique dynamics usually varying with gender. The next child creates a new system of four members and more complex dynamics with sibling rivalry among others. The next, another new system. In short, all the children have grown up in a different family and each family has different dynamics. You may have read or know of the wealth of research that has been done in seeking to establish how behaviours are influenced by placement and gender in the family. It not you could find it interesting. I was having coffee with two colleagues, both highly-qualified Ph.D. psychologists, and they were discussing worrying family problems that they were facing in their own lives. As they did this, I drew systems diagrams, illustrating what they were describing. I then showed them the diagrams and suggested possible solutions. They were blown away! Not only did the diagrams visually show the problems, but showed them simply and clearly, as well as the means to possibly resolve them. Neither of them was familiar with General Systems Theory but were excited with how they could apply its concepts in their practices.

If you extend this thinking to understanding organisations you can see how a new member joining a team or department creates a new team or department, as a new child creates a new family. This is much more profound if the new member is a manager or leader. Look around, and you can see how taking a systems approach gives new insights, perspectives and understanding in a host of organisational situations.

Isomorphism: Von Bertalanffy also introduced the concept of isomorphism, which highlights the similarity in organisational principles between diverse types of systems, such as biological, social, and mechanical ones. Simple examples I have already used illustrate this.

Entropy

Strongly associated with Systems Theory is the concept of Entropy. In physics it represents the unavailability of a system's thermal energy for conversion into work, often seen as the degree of randomness or disorder. In a broader context it is the lack of order or predictability in a system or it's gradual decline into disorder or even death. We can envisage a market in which entropy reigns supreme. In Germany, in 1923, the Mark exchange rate with the US Dollar hit 1 trillion, and a wheelbarrow of money would not buy a loaf of bread. This was an example of entropic inflation. Another example is Planet Earth. Earth is an open system. It relies for its survival on the energy input from the sun. If the sun switched off, Earth would immediately move towards entropy and death, and at a distant future time, though for a different reason, this will happen.

There is a difference between this example, and those seen everywhere else, where the impact or influence is in both directions.

This is because Earth is so small relative to the sun that Earth's impact on it is virtually unmeasurable.

It is worth looking at a variety of very simple examples of open systems and how all-pervasive the theory is. This is why I was so awestruck when I discovered it. I have been ever since, seeing its value equally as a tool of analysis, understanding and prediction or forecasting.

Some years ago, I bought shares in an Australian company whose focus was designing equipment to treat sleep apnoea and associated disorders. It proved a sound investment, until just recently, as I write, it suffered a near 30% reduction in its share value almost overnight. Having experienced steady growth over some years I was stunned. What disaster had happened? On investigation there was no obvious disaster.

A pharmaceutical company named Novo Nordisk had developed a drug for Type 2 diabetes called Ozempic or Wegovy. It was found to have an amazing side effect in weight loss. Everyone was getting it for this reason and the poor type 2 diabetes sufferers were having trouble getting it for their diabetes. This was the reason my shares had lost 30% in value almost overnight. The question is why? And here is where GST comes into play. If large numbers of overweight and obese people started using Ozempic, their numbers would decline. A major cause of sleep apnoea is being overweight or obese, so a decline in people with obesity could cause a decline in sleep apnoea. A decline in sleep apnoea could cause a decline in demand for devices to treat sleep apnoea. The possible impact on company profits was seen as sufficient to drop the share price by 30%. I thought this a grossly exaggerated response as Ozempic is very expensive, its effects plateau, it must be taken forever to maintain results and it comes with many side effects. So, I reasoned that the share had become an exceptionally good buy, and it should bounce back strongly, and it did! Dramatic changes can happen overnight in this digital age and companies that were world leaders fail. Nokia is just one example It had over 48% of the global mobile market in 2007 but only 4% in 2013, when it sold its mobile phone business to Microsoft. This was courtesy of Steve Jobs and Steve Wozniak who launched the first iPhone in 2007 and took over as world number one.

As I write, it has just occurred to me that a new major force in doing GST analysis are the social media platforms. These can be a force in almost every company's environment. A post by one widely followed influencer, say on TikTok, can damage and make or break a product or company. The problem with this is that what could appear on a platform, and when it could appear, are unpredictable, thus difficult to factor in, and yet can result in an overnight success or a death sentence. There are companies willing to pay significant sums to successful influencers on media platforms to sponsor their product, or bag and criticise their competitors, or both. This is facilitated as the rules for conduct and control on these media platforms seem almost non-existent. Now with AI, social media impact is exploding at an exponential rate, and it is becoming almost impossible to ascertain what is true and what is false, including visuals and voices. Managers at all levels are having to confront this. Understanding organisations now requires one to be more aware of the company's broader environment, and what could be happening due to social media influencers or cyber criminals. These are other sources of entropy.

On a global scale, we can see enumerable examples of systems theory at play. We can see that across our environments, damage to habitats, deforestation, oceanic warming, ocean current change, glacial and sea ice shrinkage are all interacting and creating climate extremes. These can lead to flora and fauna losses or extinctions, potentially massive movements of climate refugees, and what appears to be a tipping point in climate, where such changes become irreversible. It is not widely known, but, in the 1950's Australian scientists, notably Graeme Pearman, warned Prime Minister Bob Menzies of the risks they saw of a warming climate in Australia. They had been measuring the carbon dioxide in the air, noted its significant increase, and discovered it was occurring world-wide. Finally, seventy years later, and arguably too late, we are finally seeing accelerating action to address our increasing carbon footprint.

These climate-related issues illustrate the first three principles of GST: holism, interdependence and interdisciplinary relations.

Using GST as a tool of analysis or prediction can be shown visually by illustrating the relationship of all the interacting elements in a map. This will be like a mind map, where a product, an industry or a device is the focal entity. You identify all the elements in the environment that affect the focal organisation. Then look at how those environmental elements affect the organisation and how they are affected by the organisation.

Brainstorming or similar activities in a team are a great way of doing this but make sure you have a variety of knowledge, skills and attributes in your team, as is done in the Delphi Technique. This is necessary as there are many research studies showing that if you have a problem engineers will see an engineering problem, accountants a financial problem and human resource people a people problem, with their solutions often limited to the same vein!

You then need to take the further step of looking at what can affect the elements in the environment that you have identified. This can be a considerable undertaking. If we look at my share example, we would have had obesity as one of the key elements. In taking the next step we would have looked at what environmental factors influence obesity. In doing this we would have considered factors that both increase and decrease obesity. In this category we could list diets, junk food, dietary supplements, surgical procedures such as gastric banding or gastric balloons, and medications. If we were thorough, we would have come up with so-called miracle drugs like Ozempic and Wegovy.

Then, by looking at the anticipated major market for these we may well have concluded our sleep apnoea devices could face a significantly reduced market. Someone did do this, and this is why the shares plunged. There may now be computer programs or clever algorithms that can quickly apply GST, though I still think it needs a human to draw what can become quite complex, interactive environmental maps.

Two recent internationally significant events also illustrate how GST can be used to analyse, explain and forecast probable outcomes. The first of these was Covid; some countries did far better modelling and had far better outcomes than others. The second is the Russian invasion of Ukraine. It has caused massive disruptions to society as well as agriculture, energy and military hardware markets, impacting economies throughout the world. Quite simple GST analysis could have quickly forecast both the intended and unintended outcomes. This was no doubt done by those with vested interests in outcomes.

It does seem that with the multiplicity of worldwide international climate-related and geological events, allied to political upheavals in Africa, Europe, South America, and indeed the USA, we are seeing an entropic environment. This is illustrated by increasing conflict in the Middle East, Africa, Asia, South America and Europe. All these will likely lead to further and increased international instability and consequences. Being future oriented with long range decision making is becoming increasingly important and increasingly challenging.

It is evident that GST and its associated thinking is relevant to virtually every area of research and understanding. It has become an increasingly valuable approach to analysing and understanding the changing relationships and dynamics within and between systems of all kinds. This analysis and understanding are essential in our increasingly interconnected, interdependent and rapidly changing world.

Just reflect briefly on the pre-industrial world prior to the 18th century, and the industrial revolution that started in England around 1760. Almost every country was largely self-sustaining. International trade was in items such as spices, dyes, furs, metals and cloth or darker trades in opium and people. Problems in any country, no matter its size, other than opium or people, had negligible impact outside that country's boundaries, unless it led to war. Concepts of competitive advantage and specialisation progressively emerged, along with increased trade. This latter was facilitated by building of new steamships and steam locomotives, increasing and accelerating communications by sea and rail. This, along with other advances in the steam powered Industrial Revolution, saw rapid and progressive changes from independence to increasing interdependence between countries.

This has escalated to the stage where our interdependence is getting out of control. The increase in dramatic events and upheavals across different regions on Planet Earth suggest that, as indicated earlier, we are seeing an accelerated progression towards uncertainty and entropy. This makes understanding and managing organisations more complex.

Culture

This is such an enormous subject. It starts with the advent of homo sapiens and explores the origins, nature, variations and behaviours within human diversity. There is a wealth of literature on culture and its many expressions in books on exploration, invasion, sociology, anthropology, and archaeology, among others. These have informed and entertained readers, fascinated to learn of cultures distant and disparate from their own. They described the varied lifestyles, rituals, beliefs, authority structures, behaviours, customs and traditions practiced by others.

Organisational culture was first introduced as a concept by Elliot Jaques in his 1951 book "The Changing Culture of a Factory". It was very controversial at the time and remains controversial. However, it would be difficult to find any text on organisations and management since then that does not include significant culture related content. Indeed, despite the controversy that originally surrounded it, we find most organisations place it high on their action or understanding agendas. It is now widely accepted that organisation culture, however defined or described, has a major influence on organisational adaptability, innovation, and success.

As outlined, culture refers to the shared patterns of behaviours, beliefs, values, customs, traditions, and social norms that are learned and transmitted within a particular society or group. You probably haven't considered it, but animal groups also have cultures. The study of their behaviour is Ethology and is surprisingly relevant to our behaviour in many ways. David Attenborough has wonderfully illustrated this. Culture encompasses the full range of human activities. These include language, arts, cuisine, social interactions, rituals, and ways of life. Culture shapes people's identities and influences the way we perceive the world, interact with others, and interpret our experiences. It plays a key role in shaping societies and communities, as well as influencing individual behaviour and the full range of decision-making processes. How does this relate to the concept of organisational culture that Jaques discussed? Unsurprisingly, it is a direct relationship, as a given organisation is just a subset or a group within a broader culture. So how can we define organisational culture?

Organisational culture refers to the shared values, beliefs, customs, and behaviours that exist within an organisation and shape its internal work environment and its boundary management. It includes the organisation's mission, vision, goals, and the overall way in which employees interact and work together, and deal with both clients and suppliers. Organisational culture plays a crucial role in determining the atmosphere, work ethic, and overall effectiveness of an organisation. It influences employee morale, communication, team spirit, innovation, risk-taking, productivity, decision-making, and the overall success of the company. An organisation's culture is reflected in its communication styles, leadership approach, operating principles, ethics, trust and risk profiles, employee practices, and the loyalty of the company to its members and vice versa. In short it is all embracing and influencing,

This definition infers that a given organisation is a monoculture. Nothing could be further from the truth, except in the smallest companies. The larger an organisation becomes, the more complex the organisational culture becomes across many different dimensions. They even develop interesting tribal like cultures like those associated with primates and many ancient and still existing societies. This is not simply associated with having a multicultural workforce. It results from the different hierarchies, goals, roles, functions, people and structures. All of these enable and foster differing cultures to emerge and flourish. Frequently, this is not recognised or understood at a senior management level. They generally, and their cultural change programs, tend to think in terms of an overarching monoculture. The leaders of an organisation and their behaviour do have the most profound influences on the broad organisational culture. However, subordinate to this, but equally important, are the different role and function related cultures in different departments or divisions. Just think about it for a moment! Would you expect to confront the same culture at the board and shop floor levels, or in sales and finance departments? Cultural variables such as language, dress, values and social activities are frequently very different, apart from those associated with the different roles.

The Diesel Locomotive Workshop

I was asked by one of my master's students, who was a human relations manager, to see if I could help sort out a festering problem in a diesel locomotive workshop in West Australia. The locomotives are critical infrastructure as they haul millions of tonnes of iron ore daily, from inland to the port facility for shipment overseas. The importance of these locomotives is evident in the sheer numbers, with some 300-400 operating in the Pilbara region. Maintenance of them is thus essential to ensuring continuous daily iron ore shipments.

The problems in this maintenance workshop seemed to have originated in the appointment of a new general manager. He had introduced a system where people had to clock on and off and stated that, for a range of activities, his knowledge of them and his approval were prerequisites. In short, he had introduced an authoritarian structure and process. Previously, the diesel mechanics, fitters and others had worked as autonomous teams without such controls. They naturally resented and resisted their introduction. This was recognised by the new general manager who responded with more control measures to show who was boss. The outcome was a strained and not happy workplace, with staff working to rules and engaging in passive resistance. As a result, productivity was declining, absenteeism was on the increase. A combative atmosphere pervaded the place, and human resources feared the loss of vital staff.

I arrived on site, got introduced around, was given unrestricted access to personnel by the general manager, and started talking with different mechanics and fitters. It was clear that they had no respect at all for the new manager. They had become increasingly cohesive, and far more mutually supportive to fight this threat to their independent, and highly effective culture. If you wanted to draw a picture to illustrate this there would have been a small circle for the manager, the large circle for the main group at some distance, and barbed wire in between. Without open communications between the two entities the outcome was a cold war. One of Winston Churchill's famous sayings was "meetings to jaw-jaw are far better than war-war". Our workshop is a case in point.

After talking with most of the staff and the manager, it was clear that the rift was major and worsening, but I'd not got any real underlying clues as to why. I decided to have a quick meal and then spend the whole night with the night shift.

It turned out to be a good decision. They were happy to be involved and talk far more freely. The night shift had a very different culture, as the manager and admin staff were all at home. The top of the pyramid had been cut off and moved away. I was told that other consultants had arrived previously, but none had worked with the night shift. The fact I'd been ready to do this had accorded me credibility and trust. While I learnt a great deal that night, the critical piece of information was related to the manager's previous career. It turned out that he had no experience with diesels motors of any kind, and especially not massive diesel locomotives. It had been discovered he was a washing machine mechanic, who had moved up in his company to be a general manager. If you look at status and cultures in the field of mechanics, near the top would be diesel mechanics, and the top of those would be big diesel locomotive mechanics. There was absolutely no way that a washing machine mechanic could be the legitimate heir to a diesel locomotive empire. The two cultures were light years apart and irreconcilably different. The decision required by senior management was clear; they needed a legitimate heir to the diesel locomotive empire. This illustrates how important culture can be and even more importantly, it shows any appointee to a new managerial role should be seen to have a legitimate right to the role by the people they will be managing.

The Team Dilemma

A common objective of organisations is to encourage the development of strong teams and team spirit, often seen as a cultural imperative. This can be a double-edged sword that you need to be aware of. The teams need to be well led, by staff accepted by the team as leaders. In this case strong teams can be great assets. Conversely, if you have strong teams and negative leadership, the team can and often does unite against the leader, with negative cultural and performance outcomes for the enterprise, as in the Diesel Locomotive case. There is a wealth of research confirming this, and it needs to be recognised. If it is not recognised and not acted on, as in so many cases, the rule of unintended consequences will reign supreme.

The Nurses

I was privileged to be a tutor in management to the first group of nurses enrolled in a new nursing degree. The tutorial group comprised the heads of nursing in all the major hospitals in a major city in Australia. The only reason they were studying for a degree was that the government had decreed that to be able to be promoted to senior positions in public hospitals, and the public health system, you had to have a degree.

The nurses were the most amazing students I've ever known, so highly motivated with all wanting a distinction or a credit pass as a minimum. I must describe walking into my first tutorial to give you some idea of their culture. I had just introduced myself when one member of the tutorial group said, *"And we don't want any fucking bullshit from you, David"*. It turned out that this nurse was head of nursing at a major emergency hospital. She had been imprisoned by the Japanese in Singapore during WWII and had survived the notorious Changi prison. She was an absolute legend. Even doctors were fearful, walking on tip toes when near her. In her domain all were very careful in her presence to not incur her wrath as she didn't suffer fools gladly!

We had fantastic tutorials; in one of them, two extremely interesting perspectives on hospital cultures emerged. Hospitals all have complex cultures. These are hierarchical within the administration and role related with doctors, nurses, ward attendants, caterers, cleaners and so on all having distinct cultures, so quite a matrix and a strongly multicultural one. We were discussing shifts and discovered there were three different shift cultures for nurses. These all principally related to their decision-making ability. The three shifts were day shift, afternoon/evening shift and night shift. The shift-related decision rules were. Thou shall not, thou may, and thou shall. So, decisions nurses were not allowed to make in the day shift became a possibility in the afternoon/evening shift and mandatory in the night shift. As you can see, this adds further cultural variables to an already complex culture.

I found this extremely interesting, guessing and later confirming, there were probably similar variables in other institutions, as there had been in the diesel mechanics example above. In the same discussions, one nurse said, "At night, I feel as though a weight has been removed from my shoulders." Suddenly I saw a picture in my mind. I then drew the classical organisational triangle on the board and chopped of the top third, drawing it again adjacent to the chopped off triangle. There you are, I said. That is the weight off your shoulders. The small triangle shows that most doctors and all the administrators have gone home.

That is the weight off your shoulders. I had never visualised this before, but it beautifully represented what had occurred and explained the feeling. This is an example of when trying to understand organisations you need to step back, look at what is going on, try to find an explanation, and see if you can draw a picture to illustrate it. Use your amazing right brain!

Using Pictures to Illustrate and Understand.

In the above example, as with my two psychologist friends, I drew a picture that illustrated the issue and got immediate understanding. There is the old saying that a picture is better than a thousand words. Also, we process and store pictures in our right brain hemisphere. Our right brain is highly efficient and capable of remarkable recall. The most common example of this is how easily we recall faces of persons, but not their names that went off to the left hemisphere. Moreover, it's a common feature of memory training to associate words with pictures. I used this very effectively with students. To facilitate the recall of chunks of knowledge. We would develop an acronym for it, and then a picture that illustrated the acronym. The picture would become the note. With one class we used this method for a whole semester. The result, in their exam, was twenty-two distinctions from twenty-four students.

This also tends to confirm that you really don't need to be that bright to succeed in most university degrees. You just need a good memory or memory technique. It certainly helped me and many of my students!

What I'm suggesting is that you should see if you can draw a picture that illustrates what is happening. For example, one that I routinely used for groups is to draw one large circle representing the group, and the on the circumference draw ovals showing to what extent group members are really involved in the group.

This can range from ovals totally within the circumference, to shapes totally outside and anything crossing the circumference in between. Those fully inside may be too involved and subordinate to the group, while those fully outside may show no interest in or commitment to the group and could potentially be major disruptors. Another thing you can try, is to draw the way you think your organisation is really structured. There will be no straight lines. But you may draw lines for one department with one or more bulges pushing into adjacent departments illustrating how this department imposes its presence on other departments. You will be really surprised how drawing a picture, or making a model, brings things to life.

Once with a group of students, early in a semester, I gave them each a bundle of straws and box of pins and asked them to make a model of themselves. They then had to explain to their fellow students how and why it represented them. The results and outcomes were remarkable. I'll just describe two. The first was a mature woman, say 40 years old, who worked in the prison system. She just made a triangle with three straws pinned together. In one corner was one pin, while the other two corners or vertices both had multiple pins. In describing this she said that she felt isolated and a loner, represented by the single pin. She felt, isolated in both her work and social groups, these groups being shown by the multiple pins in the other two corners.

There are two points that need to be made here. It takes a lot of guts for someone who is a loner to open-up like this in a public arena, so why was she able to do so? Prior to her, three other more outgoing students had described their models, with great interest and positive comments or thoughts expressed by other students. There had been no hurtful laughter, no criticism and no negative comments. This had shown that it was a safe environment in which to express thoughts, feelings and emotions. It is such groups that can weave wonderful magic for members. The other students identified with her feelings and emotions, and immediately came to her aid. The outcome was that she posted in her workplace, on butcher's paper, her feelings of isolation and emotions expressed in writing. She gave us feedback on what the outcome had been in her workplace. It had been remarkable. She was so excited to be telling us and was a changed person. Her work colleagues were stunned to discover she felt isolated. Most thought that she had purposely been reclusive, had wanted to keep herself to herself, and had behaved accordingly towards her. Her action changed all that and she was now a happy member of her work group. This experience was also replicated in her home social group. Her pin was now among the others in both corners of her triangle. This also illustrates how damaging and dysfunctional false perception can be, and how having the courage to express feelings and emotions can have profound outcomes. It also illustrates how profoundly individual's lives can be changed through simple behavioural exercises conducted in a safe learning environment. I must emphasise that it needs to be a safe, and risk-free learning environment, if you want true, full and open participation. It is also the environment you should seek in your work organisation. This example illustrates how important it is to individuals and the organisation.

The second example is a quick one. One student made a raft. In her description she said she felt like the raft and was drifting at the whim of wind and ocean currents without the means to get control. I could identify with this as there was a time in my life when I felt the same! To cut a long story short, we later went out together, and many years later are still doing so, and have done some wonderful drifting together, but with the ability to control where and how!

I'd like to go back to the need for a safe learning environment and revisit the Tavistock group exploratory conference. Having a safe learning environment is vitally important, whatever the learning context. A member of our group was a leading clinical psychiatrist from Sweden. He was dressed from head to foot in black. Black shoes and socks, black trousers, and a black roll neck skivvy. He had a close crew cut and rimless spectacles. For three days he sat in our group, observing what was taking place but saying and contributing nothing, despite attempts to include him. On day four there was an opportunity for him to speak on the topic for discussion at that stage. He started to talk and then talked for a long time in a torrent of feelings and emotions. In this time, we heard the story of his hidden inner life. It was a story of his self-doubts, his deemed inadequacies, and other behavioural barriers that kept him socially isolated. He told us he was even unable to have close and warm relationships with his wife and his children. Here was a leading clinical psychiatrist. Someone who spent his life helping others with mental illness and serious behavioural problems but was unable to help or seek help for himself.

What had happened in the group that resulted in him unburdening himself, how did the group react, and what was the outcome for him?

After three days of observing how the group worked, and how it treated its members, our psychiatrist had finally decided that it was a safe group. A group in which you could take risks and discuss things you had never ever before been willing to share, even with close professional colleagues, and even with your wife and other family members or social friends.

Our group fulfilled his expectations. We all listened avidly and without interruption. We all recognised the risks that our member was taking, and realised what possibilities it created for us as individuals and as a group. It also showed what a great culture our group had developed in only three days!

When he finished talking there was a silence, and then the group started its therapy work, showing acknowledgement of his risk, affinity, empathy, insight, support, and warmth. From that time, he became a lively, enthusiastic and active participant in our group and in the collective social activities.

I feel certain that everyone reading this can identify with the suppressed issues experienced by our psychiatrist. He was incredibly lucky to have attended the conference and been a member of such a group. I say this, as other groups at the same conference developed quite diverse cultures. None it seemed, had reached the advanced evolutionary state as had ours. On his return to Sweden, our psychiatrist contacted some of us in the group. He told us he could not believe how his life had changed. He described it as a re-birth. His relationships with his wife and family were wonderful, and not only was he enjoying his work and relationship with his colleagues far more, but he felt he was a much better psychiatrist!

A look at membership of our group will give an idea of the mix. There were fourteen members with thirteen men and one woman. It included: Managing Director of Unilever, Spain. Medical Director of Volvo, Sweden. Chief Engineer of Courage Brewery, UK. General Manager British Leyland, UK. Two prominent authors of management textbooks, USA. Director of Human Relations-Shell International. Netherlands. Director of a United Nations Division, Belgium. National Clinical Lead for Psychology NHS, UK.

It was quite remarkable how well we operated as a group in a short space of time. The development process may have been accelerated by my role as a facilitator. Group behaviour was a key element of my studies, and I knew the role I could play! I was extremely fortunate to attend this conference, courtesy of my Tavistock supervisor. It proved to be one of the most interesting and influencing experiences that I have enjoyed.

Idiosyncratic and Extreme Cultures

Most organisational cultures are not drastically different to the host culture and evolve along with the host cultures. However, there are exceptions. These are where certain organisational structures and cultures can become independent of their host culture and yet have almost the same culture in every country in the world despite the differing host cultures.

An example is prisons. Prisons in almost every country in the world, with notable exceptions in Scandinavian countries, have remarkably similar systems, cultures, norms of behaviour, rules, regulations, and punishments that are independent of the host culture. Some are truly frightening. Who remembers Midnight Express, The Shawshank Redemption or Papillon?

We have all heard, seen, or read of the risks of physical and sexual abuse, common in both male and female prisons in virtually every country. We have also seen or read of brutal and inhuman punishments meted out such as in the movies mentioned. But there are even worse unintended consequences from punishment regimes. I read a great research study from France. The researchers had got the prisoners to work out a system that guaranteed the anonymity of any contributor. As a result, this was the first study to get the truth of what really went on in the prison. It was fascinating reading, but the main unrecognised and unintended consequence of the punishment routine that I remember was this. As in most prisons, regular searches were conducted to check for weapons manufactured or concealed by prisoners. In the prison, the penalty for attacking or injuring another prisoner was nominal, but the discovery of a weapon was at the top of the list of serious offences as it could be used to attack a guard. The penalties in this case were severe, with the certainty that the offending prisoner would be savagely beaten by guards, then isolated in a cell only 2 metres by one metre and further brutalised. The prisoners, as a result, had their own solution to avoid weapon carrying punishments. Before the weapon, often a knife was, discovered on a prisoner, they would attack and use it on another prisoner, severely wounding and, in some cases, killing them.

This illustrates an important and frequent issue to consider. When new policies, rules, or regulations get promulgated, beware the unintended consequences or collateral damage! Using a systems approach in formulation and evaluation can lead to a far lower risk of undesired, unanticipated, or untoward outcomes.

The Brickworks – A Horticulture Culture

One of my good friends was the chief executive of a merchant bank that had acquired a rural brickwork manufacturer as part of a larger corporate takeover. It was not a very profitable business, and it was not a good fit with the other businesses in their portfolio. The plan was to see if it could be made sufficiently profitable to on-sell, and my friend asked me if I was interested in managing it to this end. I knew nothing about brick manufacturing, but the basic principles are a constant and so I accepted the challenge.

The following week I drove the 400 kilometres to the site, met the previous owners, and had a crash course in brick making. It was a vintage operation, making bricks the same way they had been for hundreds of years. Digging out the clay, using moulds to form the bricks and firing them in wood burning brick kilns using timber supplied by local mills. Unlike most "clay" bricks made now, made from combinations of clay, shale and other minerals with not much clay, these bricks were all clay. Different clay mixes and different firing processes produced a wonderful range of earthy or woodland colours.

After considerable discussions about production, sales, and finance it was clear that with plenty of clay, production could easily be increased. The main problem was lack of sales and cash flow plus impending cost increases in wood to fire the kilns. With this done, it was time to be introduced to and meet the employees numbering some hundred and twenty. We met in a local hall with beer and wine supplied by the company. They were a typical country crew, males of all shapes, sizes, and demeanours, and all wearing jeans or boiler suits with heavy check woollen shirts and well-worn sports shoes or Japanese safety boots (aka thongs).

The air was blue with smoke and the characteristic smell of marijuana enveloped me. I was having a lively conversation with Alan, clearly the accepted leader, who was smoking a joint the size of a cigar. He, offered to roll me one. I declined, as I could never inhale smoke, so he offered a hash brown alternative, a local culinary specialty for which they were famous, along with truffles. I had to raise with Alan the issue of safety as wood fired kilns are major hazards, especially when our people walked on and in them! He told me that if I planned to introduce any alcohol or drug testing then I might as well close the plant down. He confirmed close to one hundred percent of our people routinely enjoyed both on a daily or at least weekly basis. All home grown, much home brewed or home cooked.

At the same time, he told me there had never been an accident requiring more than band aids or paracetamol. If you can't beat them, join them, and so I did, on the understanding that we had never had our conversation. I later became highly educated in the best practice cultivation of natural and hydroponic marijuana and the wide variety of butters, oils, hash browns or muffins used as dietary or medicinal supplements. However, I still had a business to run. Management structure was simple. It was Alan and me. I agreed with Alan to increase production progressively by 50% to 100%, well within our capacity, and opened a sales office, with a sales manager in the state capital. Demand leapt, particularly after I discovered amazingly, that I could backload trucks 4000 kilometres to major eastern states cities at the same cost per tonne as the local deliveries of bricks, and thus compete with their brickworks.

Sales and production were moving ahead nicely when I got a call from the trade union covering our industry. They wanted to visit and get our employees to sign up and unionise the site. I invited them to come the following week, then discussed it with Alan and the implications for their way of life. The union representatives duly arrived and gave their pitch. Alan then asked for a show of hands for those who wanted to join the union. None went up. Alan then told the union representatives that they had their answer, and they had 5 minutes to get off the site or be thrown off, and to not come back. The union men started blustering about rules, rights, and agreements when Alan said. "Right lads! let's escort these gentlemen off site." They all rose as one and the union men ran for their car, with their audience in pursuit, spinning their wheels on the gravel as they drove off. That was the last we saw or heard of them! We went back to standard operating procedures.

Production and sales were up substantially. We reached a stage where demand exceeded our capacity to supply, despite price increases. All these led to positive cash flows and significant net profit. The particularly good return on investment made the business eminently saleable. I had ordered equipment from Sweden that could continuously fire the kilns on wood chips or sawdust that was plentiful in supply and reduce the reliance on good timber. This would also further reduce energy and labour costs. My work was over. A buyer had come forward and a sale completed. It had been a fun and challenging project. I left after a celebratory evening with the crew and gifts of local specialties, wondering how the new owners would deal with the rather special plant-based organisational culture.

Simple Cultural Changes

Cultural change does not have to be organisation wide, nor difficult to implement. Small changes can have very rewarding outcomes. As a manager in a major engineering company, I walked into our large warehouse, and as I did so I noticed a storeman grab a broom and start sweeping. I immediately identified with this behaviour, having been guilty of the same behaviour, as I am sure have most people at some time. So that you are not seen to be idle, you pretend to be engaged in work. I knew from my experience that this was associated with an unpleasant feeling of guilt. I wanted to eliminate this, and so called a meeting of our storemen and women. I proposed that a section of the store be converted into a lounge area, with comfortable sofa and chairs and refrigerator, plus tea and coffee facilities. Staff could relax and enjoy these any time they were without a current task. In return I asked that when needed to work extra time, to get last orders out or receive goods, that they would do it and not claim overtime. Without exception they agreed. The following day staff cleared an area and arranged the furniture, fridge and tea and coffee facilities I had purchased. As a result of the change and limited expenditure, our overtime costs went down by over 50%, the guilt was eliminated, and there was a lot of laughter and social interaction, with coffee plus cakes brought and shared. The one-off cost to the company was nominal but the outcome culturally, behaviourally, and financially was terrific and ongoing. An absolute win-win requiring no consultants and no rocket science, just observation, recognition, and action.

Organisational Psychopaths and How They Behave

I have recently read interesting research about members of organisations, who originally would have been classed as sociopaths, but are now seen more as psychopaths. As I have said previously, understanding organisations means getting to understand the complex behaviours of individuals and groups, and their interactions. This requires you to really look around and observe behaviours like a behavioural analyst.

You need to be sensitive to undesirable behavioural changes. Disruptive forces may suddenly seem to be at play. Mistrust can seem to have evolved, while dysfunctional changes in the culture or subversive acts can also seem to have taken place. If any or all these changes are occurring, you should take a very close look at people in the organisation, especially more recent appointments. In population studies, and other meta-analysis research, the percentage of psychopaths in adult populations has ranged from around 1.5% to 4%. So, they will be present in most organisations of larger size. Let us have a closer look at psychopathy. I am sure everyone who has spent some time in the workforce will know of a psychopath. Typically, psychopaths are charming and gregarious when they join an enterprise but over time they progressively undermine and criticise other staff members and can happily destroy the organisation that employs them.

Psychopathy is a condition characterised by the absence of empathy and the blunting of other affective states. Callousness, detachment, and a lack of empathy enable psychopaths to be highly manipulative, with absolutely no consideration for anyone other than themselves. Nevertheless, psychopathy is among the most difficult disorders to spot. Psychopaths can appear normal, even charming. Underneath, they lack any semblance of conscience, and their antisocial nature often inclines them towards criminality, though they would not see it as such. Of course, they think they are always right, even if their views are proven to be false. They are also masters at reading other people. Then by flattering and manipulating them, by telling them what they want to know and what they want to hear, they get them on their side. This is why you absolutely cannot go to a superior to complain about being harassed or bullied by a psychopath. They will already have anticipated this and ingratiated themselves with their superior. They will already have suggested to them, that if anyone should come to them complaining, that it is because they had to be reprimanded for poor work. So immediately you, the victim, are believed to be the one at fault, not the psychopath. The only legal and effective way to deal with a harassing or invective psychopath is to leave the group or organisation.

Psychopaths spark popular fascination, perhaps originating in Alfred Hitchcock's famous movie *Psycho*. Meanwhile, for psychoanalysts, they present clinical conundrums. Adult psychopathy has been shown to be resistant to treatment. Some programs exist that attempt to treat callous, unemotional youths in hopes of preventing them from maturing into psychopaths. However, recent research suggests that these young people inherit the criteria for being a psychopath. Due to their brain structure, and the fact that it's integral to their personality, they are quite likely doomed to become adult psychopaths. As I have suggested, in recent times, it's been recognised that brain anatomy, genetics, and a person's environment may all contribute to the development of psychopathic traits. Now it seems there are even early brain scans that can determine if a person is indeed clinically a psychopath.

One widely thought of as an example of psychopathic behaviour is Donald Trump. Apparently, most people who meet him personally find him very personable and quite charming. However, one must only look at his time serving as POTUS and his behaviour once he was no longer President to see this is a facade. It was The Washington Post who recorded that he had told 783 outright lies as President. A further example was his apparent support for the invasion of the White House by his followers. This was unprecedented in America's history. Then we had the constant and ongoing claim that he had won the election, and that it had been stolen from him through fraudulent voting systems. Associated with this was the brazen attempt to alter voting outcomes in Georgia, despite the claims of counting errors being totally and irrefutably discounted. He allegedly stole government top secret documents and worse, allegedly disclosed top military secrets to unauthorised personal and business associates. He blamed others for every failure of his presidency and there were countless failures. He is now facing something in the order of 90 criminal indictments and responds to all by saying that all the charges are fabricated. In addition, he claims the attorneys or judges, who are laying the charges, are incompetents who should have no role in the judiciary or justice system. Can you imagine having someone like Donald Trump in your organisation? The chances are, if it is a reasonable sized organisation, you already have, but hopefully not as extreme!

Consultants – Don't Trust Them!

There is an absolute and fundamental reason why you should use consultants with care, and only after you have drawn up a watertight contract, detailing the role and responsibilities of the consultant, and including major penalties, should they breach any aspect of the contract. Even then, they can probably breach the contract without you being aware of it. But what is the fundamental problem I have alluded to? It is that the intrinsic goals of the consultants are directly in conflict with the goals of the organisation.

Let us have a look at psychiatrists. If a person comes to a psychiatrist with a mental health issue, the proper ethical and target outcome should be realised when the patient no longer needs the psychiatrist and walks away saying "I don't need you anymore". However, it is clearly in the psychiatrist's financial and personal interests to maintain the patient's dependence on them and derive a continuous income flow. If the psychiatrist does adopt the ethical approach and does generate healthy independence in the patient, the patient, after having been deeply dependent, tells the psychiatrist, "I do not need you. Get out of my life!" This can, apart from being financially detrimental, be seriously mentally damaging to the psychiatrist. This is why most good psychiatrists need psychiatric help from colleagues, and I speak from experience.

I can personally attest to how damaging it can be; this is why I ceased using a psychiatric model of consulting. There were two different consulting assignments where I had helped the company avoid going into liquidation, one in Australia and one in the UK. This was achieved by taking effective control of the company, as opposed to just being a consultant.

In the UK I had succeeded in avoiding insolvency and liquidation and was on the way to set a company on a sound financial footing. It was at this point of maximum dependency that I was offered the earth! This was a contract with salary package five times my current income paid into a tax-free offshore account, while living on expenses with a top range BMW. The other dependency offer in Australia, was not so generous, but still far more than double my current income plus very substantial perks. This is the dependency state in a relationship that normal consulting companies love, as it presents the opportunity to negotiate lucrative contracts. I proceeded the ethical way, avoided insolvency and liquidation, and got both companies on a really sound operating and financial footing, with people to replace me. They then no longer needed me. This resulted in my total dismissal and rejection. From being a hero, I was now a leprous outcast, and knew this would be the outcome of success. Pretty crazy when you think about it!

This was seriously damaging to my self-esteem, my self-image, and my ego; candidly, I was devastated. The damage was such that I decided I'd never accept a similar undertaking again; and I never did. However, psychiatrists constantly face this. It is a terrible situation to face; when you know that if you succeed in generating true client independence, you will suffer almost total rejection. It is much like the situation when a couple are madly in love and suddenly one calls it off, leaving the other rejected and devastated, suicidal or homicidal. In *Pygmalion*, the flower seller Eliza Doolittle is totally dependent on Professor Higgins until he has succeeded in turning her into the lady, he claimed he could. This, in behavioural terms is called the Pygmalion effect. Suddenly Eliza realises she no longer needs Professor Higgins and walks away, leaving him devastated and in disbelief. This move to independence is termed the Aphrodite effect. The relationship dynamics are the same as in the psychiatric consulting model. To reiterate, despite claims to the contrary, there is a 90% plus probability that the primary goal of consultants will be to generate dependency on their services, rather than independence of them. This intrinsically means that they will not principally be acting in the interests of their client, but their own interests.

Consulting to and Infiltrating Organisations

Let us think a bit more about consulting companies and the realisation that their financial goals put them in direct conflict with both ethical goals and the goals of the client organisation. This is a universal fact. The consulting companies want to maximise dependence on them and progressively increase this dependence until they become essential to the client's operation. The client company in outsourcing management is arguably increasing its risk, due to reliance on consultants, while failing to invest in its own independence. It can get even worse. This is when the consulting company uses or sells, information gained in confidence, to increase their client base, possibly with competitive companies, or to strengthen their existing clients' reliance on them.

Consulting companies also love to get the same or similar requirements from different companies. Once they have done all the work, research, and recommendations for one company, they can and do badge engineer it, meaning that they change the client's name, and a few variables then submit it to the new client. This is highly profitable and like a lawyer having a template for a Last Will and Testament on the computer. All that needs doing for a new client is change the names, address client specific variables, get it signed and charge your standard $1,500 plus fee.

A classic, headline-grabbing case in Australia involved one of the big four consulting companies, working with the taxation department, to develop strategies or processes to block major corporations avoiding income taxation in Australia. This avoidance was by corporations using tactics such as transfer pricing, paying massive sums to an offshore company for marketing, using complex financial structures or taking loans at remarkably high interest rates from offshore related entities. In every case, the strategies are designed and developed so profits were transferred to and made in low tax or tax haven countries, with Ireland and the Netherlands being popular ones.

What they were doing was totally amoral, but it was enabled by current legislation and thus not classed as tax evasion, even though it clearly was in all but name. The main international culprits designing these schemes for companies, are the big four accounting and consulting companies because, as in so many aspects of Australian enterprise, we have an effective oligopoly. All four of these companies would be equally guilty of seeking to maximise client dependency on them. The only difference between them would likely be, the extent to which individuals would suppress ethics, honesty and trust in their activities in pursuit of the god Mammon.

Understanding Abstruse Organisational Behaviour

As we have seen, to understand organisations, you must often go behind the veil, lift the curtain, open closed doors, venture into forbidden territory, go where no man has gone before, and imagine the unimaginable. You must do this to realise, understand and explain much of what happens in them. Even then, be ready to be surprised. You really do have to wear the mantle of a detective and I am minded of the old maxim of Sherlock Holmes that, when you have excluded the impossible, whatever remains, however improbable, must be the truth or the cause. Would you like an example?

Anomalous Educational Career Path

Among life's great mysteries are how some people get appointed to positions in organisations where they have none of the skills, qualities and attributes required to fill the role. This is the story of one of them.

Some years ago, many of Australia's tertiary education institutions underwent a process of corporatisation in structure and role description.

Instead of a Principal we got a Managing Director, and, instead of Superintendents of Curriculum, or External Studies we got General Managers. All of this was accompanied by the benefits of company vehicle, expense accounts, credit cards and more.

In one such major educational institution, the Managing Director got his position through his family being good friends of the incumbent minister for education, being tapped on the shoulder and being told, "If you'd like this it's yours; just apply." His qualifications for the top role in this major institution, both on paper and in experience, were non-existent but nepotism prevailed. However, this story is not about him, disturbing enough though that is.

The managing director's secretary went on leave for two weeks. A temporary replacement was sought from the redundancy pool of government employees. The lucky person selected was a secretarial staff member made redundant from another ministry who duly arrived to take on her temporary role. This is where it gets a bit awkward. Our new appointee had undisclosed skills and attributes that our director found essential in the role, and soon a humorous nickname, for the temporary secretary was being bandied around.

The problem was how he could retain access to her skills and attributes when his normal secretary returned. By a fortunate coincidence, the role of General Manager Curriculum had recently been advertised; even more fortunate, there was now an available candidate, despite having no relevant skills. But there was a solution. The appropriate department was to provide an immediate qualification in management. This was done, and the secretary from the redundancy pool was suddenly the new General Manager Curriculum of a major educational institution, along with all the benefits that role included. Remarkably, this role was retained for a considerable time, despite total disbelief from other similar institutions. Senior members of these had contacted me to ask about this General Manager whose only knowledge of curriculum, as far as they could ascertain, was how to spell it, and they weren't even sure about that. Ultimately, there was a face-saving move to nowhere until the saga could be effectively buried and moved on from.

Aviation Career Path

One of my particularly good and old friends with whom I'd travelled to and around UK and Europe and flat-shared with in London, appeared at the door of the home I lived in, at the time in Whale Beach, north of Sydney. His was a sad story. He and his family had flown to England for his marriage to a young woman who had courted him for some years. At the last minute she had cancelled it. It was all over. Roland's reaction had been to drink himself into oblivion, losing interest in career, life and everything else. His last recourse was to get back to Sydney and come to see me, helped financially by his mother. My home was a perfect rehabilitation environment: tranquil, stress-free, and beautiful.

I was more than happy to provide the home, support and companionship he needed, as we got on very easily together. He improved and developed a little social round, calling on ladies, and the occasional gentleman who supplied him with tea, coffee, scones and what have you. This lasted for about three months when I suddenly had to move 50km to the eastern suburbs of Sydney, due to geographic changes in my job. Roland came with me, but I told him he had to get a job. He did, and of all things it was packing fireworks in a fireworks factory no less. He was intelligent, bright, and quite handsome. In his mid-20s he had already been the head of a Masonic Lodge. I could not accept him packing fireworks, so I organised an interview for him with one of our major aviation companies. This company was well known, at least within the industry, for having a significant gay network. What was not so well known was that it also had a masonic network. Roland joined and, within eighteen months had received promotions into quite responsible jobs, where his salary now exceeded mine. He was an effective manager and, to cut a long story short, he eventually became head of a department and one of the most senior executives. This was thanks in no minor part to his Masonic links. He had not only been the head of a Blue Lodge but was also an office bearer in an exclusive order, with regalia making a Catholic cardinal look dowdy.

As with our education example, the traditional, formal or conventional process had been subverted, in this latter case with a positive organisational outcome. I am sure everyone who may read this has seen examples of inexplicable promotions. The bottom line is that they are not inexplicable. There is a reason or reasons for every single one. The challenge is to discover the reason, and the reasons may well be sequestered, or shrouded to shield them from discovery. This is another challenge in understanding organisations.

There was a wonderful example in one state, where a detective sergeant of the fraud squad was suddenly promoted to police commissioner. That is a serious promotion. I leave it to the reader to hazard a guess as to the reasons why that may have happened.

Successful Alternative Organisational Structures

The conventional organizational structure is the authority-based pyramid shape with the pyramid steeper or flatter according to the number of levels within it. There are successful alternatives to this so let's have a look at some.

The Basque region of Spain is known for its strong tradition of worker cooperatives and innovative cooperative models. One of the most well-known examples is the Mondragon Cooperative Corporation. It is considered the world's largest federation of worker cooperatives, and at last count comprised a voluntary association of some ninety-five independent cooperatives. Here are some of the key features of Mondragon and its innovative cooperative model.

Mondragon Corporation was founded in 1956 in the town of Mondragon. It is a voluntary federation of autonomous worker cooperatives that operate in various industries, including manufacturing, finance, retail, and education. These have evolved from the original single cooperative, and it is a major economic force in the Basque Country and Spain as a whole.

Mondragon is characterised by its emphasis on worker ownership and democratic decision-making. Employees, after proving themselves, can become member-owners with shares and have a say in the management and governance of their respective cooperatives. In some countries, Germany is a good example, both private and public companies frequently have participation of workers or unions in management and governance. The success of many German enterprises has often been ascribed to this.

The Mondragon system places a strong emphasis on education and training. It has its own cooperative university, Mondragon University, established in 1997. It is probably the only cooperative university in the world! It provides education, employing cooperative principles and management, and has a broad range of subjects at undergraduate and postgraduate levels.

Mondragon is guided by principles of social solidarity, and it has policies in place to promote job security and income equality among its worker-owners. The most a chief executive can earn is six times the salary of the lowest wage earner. To put this into perspective I looked at two large Australian companies. Using the most recent figures in one major mining company the CEO earned 488 times the lowest paid worker and in the other, a major conglomerate the CEO earned 228 times the lowest paid worker. Australian CEOs on average earn 55 times the minimum wage in their companies. Income disparity and associated wealth disparity are becoming major social, economic, and political issues in many democratic countries. This is causing real concern, not only for governments, but also some of the world's super wealthy. As with many things the Scandinavians have been effective and successful trailblazers of social solidity and equity policies.

Mondragon's cooperative enterprises have expanded globally, with subsidiaries and cooperative ventures in various countries. Remarkably these include the United States and China. You may like to further research Mondragon as it has lessons for aspiring business owners or managers.

Apart from Mondragon, the Basque region has seen the growth of other cooperative initiatives in areas such as agriculture, industry, and finance. The region's cooperative movement is celebrated for its innovation, sustainability, and commitment to democratic principles in the workplace. As far as I am aware, there is no comparable cooperative structure to Mondragon anywhere else. This is despite its evident success and its growth and development for over 70 years. However, it remains as an example of just what can be done to have successful organisations that promote social equality. How preferable is this to those corporations of the digital and gig economy, giving rise to social inequality, allied to job and income insecurity. If recent data is to be believed, these digital and gig organisations have also helped to foster a surge in mental health issues, especially in the young members of our population.

Another widely known example of a successful alternative organisational structure, while not as major or as dramatic as Mondragon, is that of Semco.

Ricardo Semler is a Brazilian entrepreneur and author known for his innovative approach to business management. He gained international recognition for his leadership style and the transformation of his family's business, Semco Partners. His wide recognition also resulted from his writing and publications on his approach and achievements.

Let us have a look at a few points about Ricardo Semler and his approach.

Ricardo Semler took over as CEO of Semco, a Brazilian manufacturing company, from his father in the 1980s. Under his leadership, Semco underwent a radical transformation in management practices.

Like in Mondragon, one of Semler's most notable management principles is the emphasis on employee empowerment. He implemented policies such as flexible work hours, employee-driven decision-making, and profit-sharing, giving employees a significant say in how the company was run.

Semler also introduced radical transparency within the organisation, sharing financial information and decision-making processes with employees. This transparency was designed to foster trust and collaboration.

Semler promoted a workplace democracy where employees could participate in decisions about their work, salaries, and company policies. He believed that this approach led to greater job satisfaction and productivity. As noted earlier this has been a feature of many German enterprises.

Semco reduced traditional hierarchies and eliminated middle management positions, creating a flatter organisational structure. This facilitated communications both up and down minimising opportunities for aberrant messaging.

Semco's flexible approach allowed it to adapt quickly to changing market conditions and innovate more effectively.

Semler's management philosophy at Semco proved successful, and the company experienced steady and increasing growth and profitability. While Semco would not be classed as a major corporation Semler's ideas influenced management practices in other organisations worldwide. He was also a good exemplar of leadership and leader behaviour.

If you would like to read more on his approach his books included:

Maverick: The Success Story Behind the World's Most Unusual Workplace (1993) and *The Seven-Day Weekend: Changing the Way Work Works* (2004), in which he shares his management insights and experiences.

Semler's unconventional approach to management has been both celebrated and critiqued, but it undeniably challenged traditional corporate practices in a similar vein as Mondragon. They both continue to be a source of inspiration for those interested in alternative business management models that prioritise employee well-being and autonomy.

Like Robert Townsend in Avis, Ricardo Semler was the chief executive of Semco. In his case he was also the owner so, like Townsend, had the freedom to implements any changes he wished, to any aspect of the organisation's operations. The more one looks at examples such as these, the more it becomes evident that to make such profound changes to an organisation one needs to meet a few criteria. Firstly, it is clearly far easier to undertake major changes in a private, unlisted family business. There are no shareholders who need to be convinced and minimal regulatory hurdles. In the case of a publicly listed company, the changes need to be championed, and implemented by a powerful and well backed CEO with an eye to minimising risks to the plans from awkward shareholders, or an inadvertent breach of some regulation.

When you look at the success these different organisations have achieved, not simply using economic measures, but more importantly, in a range of key social measures, you wonder why such organisations are not more widespread. Australia, in fact, has a long history of cooperatives and mutuals going back to the mid-19th century. There are at last count over 1800 cooperatives or mutuals in Australia. They range from small not for profit ones to large multi-million commercial enterprises serving national and international markets. They also have an organisation that represents them. It is the BCCM, the Business Council of Cooperatives and Mutuals. In many cases the organisations are not recognised or thought of as cooperatives or mutuals. These include the massive industry superannuation funds. The largest commercial cooperative, in terms of turnover, would be CBH in West Australia, a grain farmers cooperative with a turnover of some four billion dollars and profit some 10% of this. The unseen role of cooperatives and mutuals in Australia is evident when one sees that they have, including superannuation funds, total assets exceeding 1.5 trillion dollars. However, they differ from Mondragon and like organisations as their structure and operations follow more closely those of conventional for-profit enterprises, without comparable member involvement.

A Unique Structure

My friend John had a company with an unusual organisational structure, and some unique characteristics. It is not offered as a model nor are some of its social and cultural features recommended. However, it does illustrate, as Monty Python would say "Something completely different", and just how some organisations can and do successfully function, despite breaching almost every theoretical concept. Hang on to your seatbelts!

I remember reading a book by Charles Handy in which he described and gave names to varying organisational structures. From memory he termed the entrepreneurial structure The Web with the spider sitting at the centre controlling the web. If John's structure was a web, it was a very untidy and uncared-for web.

A Special Friend

John was one of my oldest and dearest friends. Our friendship is epitomised by my receiving a call after midnight one night. It went as follows "Hi Dave (he is the only person I let call me Dave), John here. I have got terminal lung cancer and I'm not going to let a hospital get me in its clutches, so I'm ending it tonight. Could I ask you to be here for me?" I am brought to tears as I am writing this. "Of course John my dear friend I answered, it has been a privilege to have you as a friend. Just make sure you do a good a job as you always have done in the past." I went to bed thinking of just how privileged I was, to have been asked to be there for the start of the next phase of his ongoing journey.

Back to the Beginning

John and I had first met and shared a smart apartment in Bellevue Hill with views of Sydney Harbour. At the time we both worked in the so called ethical pharmaceutical industry. However, John had discovered that every kilo of green x-ray film contained an ounce of silver and that through burning the used film and treating the fixer you could recover close to 100% of the silver. The enterprise was to become the largest silver recovery business in Australia, but it started with us burning x-ray film in a 44-gallon drum at midnight, so the acrid fumes and black smoke were silently dissipated on the refined night air of Bellevue Hill.

As the business grew beyond our nightly 44-gallon drums John purchased a factory in an inner semi-industrial suburb. In this he designed and manufactured units to electrolytically extract silver from photographic fixer. John then negotiated contracts to install these units into hospital x-Ray departments and purchase their redundant film. The way John managed his company is an illustration of how far you can go from conventional structures and policies and still have an amazing culture and successful enterprise.

Firstly, John staffed his whole operation with people who were conventionally unemployable. They comprised disabled people, people with physical imperfections, e.g. a lady with massive burn scarring, veterans with missing limbs and ex-prison inmates. This disparate group of people individually and collectively idolised John. One ex-inmate appointed himself John's minder and asked me to source some replica firearms. At the time they were still legally available in one state. This I did, and as they say about the United States presidents' guards, he would have taken a bullet for John. I could add many more interesting stories, but we are focusing on understanding organisations not very idiosyncratic or norm-breaking behaviour.

The Structureless Structure

The structure of John's company was flat, without any hierarchy at all. Everyone was equal, including John, who was accessible to anyone at any time on any subject, even though he was the owner. Everyone was equally valued, except John, as he was effectively the leader and protector of his great group of misfits who idolised him. In one sense it was a little like *The Life of Brian*, with John constantly having to declare, "I'm not the Messiah: I'm just an anarchist and social rebel." Equally there were no rules or regulations, no scheduled hours of work, no control over when employees came or left or any other records. What was known by all and respected, was that when something needed doing, no matter what, where or when, it was to be done until it was finished. John's "Just do it" preceded Nike by many years!

John's office was a large open-plan barn-like place. It was open to all and sundry at all hours. Other than the legendary Balmain Hotel, owned by Olympic legend Dawn Fraser and her partner, John's place was the next most popular local meeting place for prostitutes, pensioners and anyone seeking a bit of companionship. There were fridges full of free beer, soft drinks, mixers, and bottles of spirits scattered on shelves.

I will recount one example to illustrate what type of a person John was. One afternoon he and I were having a quiet beer when an old pensioner came in and approached us. "Why are you looking so miserable, you old prick" asked John. "It's my wife John," he said. "I've just left the doc's, and she needs an operation and no way can I afford it." "How much are we talking about," asked John. "Over $1,500," he replied. An absolute fortune to him.

At that, John reached into a pocket, pulled out a roll of notes, counted out $2,000, folded them and pushed them into the pensioner's pocket. John then cracked a beer, gave it to him and said, "Drink that, and put a smile on that ugly face, and then go get your old lady fixed up." I think you can see why John commanded so much respect and admiration. This could work in many ways. An ex-jail inmate to whom John had given a job stole silver worth about $6,000, a significant sum at the time, and disappeared from the area. The response from John's other employees was predictable; his trust had been abused. Retribution was demanded, and the call went out that this person had stolen from John, and everyone was to look for him. About two weeks later I was with John having a beer in the local pub. Two men, unknown to John, approached us "Morning John," one said. "We are friends of your friends, and we would just like you to know that we found your thief. We could not recover any funds for you, so we taught him a lesson, running him over with a forklift truck. He deserved it. Bye John!" These revelations may come as a surprise to many readers, but over my lifetime I have come across a surprising number of organisations where understanding them requires considering whether and to what extent criminal or similar elements are at play, directly or indirectly.

At the risk of being seriously politically incorrect, and stepping on dangerous ground, I will describe a few more events that pertain to John's unique culture.

One night, I received a telephone call about midnight. "Hi Dave! John here! I have chartered a 707 and I am taking all my staff for a holiday in Bangkok. The best deal I have found is for all of us to stay in an upmarket people's pleasure palace that caters for everyone. If you can make it, I would love you to join us, and you can bring anyone except your wife."

I told my wife, who laughed and said, "Typical John." From the feedback I got, everyone had a fantastic time, and all were medically checked before coming home. Do not think this latter behaviour is limited to companies like John's. I know major international corporations in motor vehicle manufacturing, finance fields and others, who routinely make such medical checks available and recommended after international symposia, reward trips, trade promotions, or junkets they conduct. Just to finish on this holiday subject, the following year there was an invitation to join John again. This time he was taking all his staff to Wrest Point Casino in Hobart and giving them $1,000 each as spending money, a far less controversial holiday! His organisational culture, structure, and everything else was a one-off but remarkably successful. However, it would not be easy to replicate as it needs a very special leader.

Enterprising Individuals

Australia has a long and colourful history of entrepreneurship, originally in farming and mining and more recently in the digital and gig economy. A little-known entrepreneur was Tom Wardle.

Sir Tom Wardle aka Tom the Cheap. A Great Australian

A good example of entrepreneurship and innovation was a supermarket business, created by Tom Wardle in Western Australia, called Tom the Cheap, with a little striped convict man as its logo. I will start by telling you how Tom ended up, and then explain how he got there. From a little corner store in the 1950's Tom Wardle became the wealthiest man in Western Australia. He was knighted to become Sir Thomas Wardle, became the Lord Major of Perth and, at the same ceremony at which I was awarded my first bachelor's degree, he was awarded a Doctor of Law for his success in breaking the cartels in Western Australia, and saving West Australians hundreds of millions of dollars annually.

Tom got his inspiration to own and operate small supermarkets from Sweden. From one little corner store Tom went looking at all the old, often run down or neglected strip retail stores scattered around Perth. This was before the development of major shopping centres when strip shopping was still prevalent. He leased the cheapest properties he could find. He fitted them all out in the cheapest conceivable way with no fancy displays, old timber shelving, wooden pallets, timber fruit and vegetable delivery crates, sacks for produce and second-hand everything including refrigeration, or else he leased. He would not even install a telephone. When staff wanted to contact his office or order anything they had to walk to the nearest public telephone. His capital outlay was thus negligible and, though his stores were all like a market stall his prices were so low that no one cared.

The public flocked to them. That was the capital side of the business, but what about the operational side? Australian supermarkets are among the most profitable in the world. They typically operate with markups exceeding the 20-25% range, with net profits around 4%. The least recognised but most potent, and importantly controllable variable, in any wholesale or retail organisation is stock turnover rate. It is the same principle that I described with pawnbrokers who charge a shilling a pound a week translating to profits of 260% per annum. If a retailer is making a margin of 4% on turnover and has a stock turnover rate of four times a year that becomes 16% gross per annum on capital. By just increasing the turnover rate to five times a year with effective inventory management the profit becomes 20% equating to a 25% profit improvement.

This principle would account for Aldi's success. Carrying just a fraction of the products carried by Coles or Woolworths, they can achieve a far better turnover rate and annual profit percentage. Now, to get back to Tom the Cheap. With a limited range and 10% markup but high turnover products, his stock turnover rate would have far exceeded the other retailers in Western Australia. Let us say for example that his margin was 5% but that he achieved a stock turn rate of 10, i.e., turning it over every 5 weeks or so. This translates to an annual 50% gross return on investment. The other major secret to Tom's success was that his amazingly rapid growth, from only one to two hundred and eight stores, was not funded with his own capital, but was almost entirely funded by his creditors.

Tom was renowned for not paying his creditors for 90 days. In those 90 days Tom, would have turned his stock over almost three times, generating some 15% in gross profits without outlaying anything. It was a fantastic business model. An obvious question is, "Why did his suppliers accept this?" The answer was simple; Tom, while renowned as a hard bargainer, was honourable. He always did pay and had become a dependable and increasingly important account to his suppliers.

I mentioned Tom's Doctor of Law. This was awarded for his cartel-busting and his very generous philanthropy.

West Australia was dominated by cartels, price-fixing was rampant, and discounting was non-existent. Consequently, many manufacturers refused to supply a price cutter like Tom with their products, but they hadn't dealt with someone like Tom. One legendary example was Bex, at the time a top selling analgesic powder. Tom's response was to get representatives of many companies travelling round the state to buy all the Bex powder they could from every retailer. Tom then sold Bex at a major discount in all his stores, obviously at a great loss, but he won the fight. Bex capitulated.

Another company who would not supply him was Cadbury. Somehow a shipment of Cadbury products had been purchased by a single buyer. This buyer turned out to be Tom, purchasing under another company name. Cadbury products were then discounted throughout Tom's stores and Cadbury capitulated. Tom successfully used similar tactics with other manufacturers. Each then discovered that he was becoming a major retail client. This was recognised by other manufacturers, who realised the business they were losing, and they started supplying Tom. Finally, he had succeeded in busting the erstwhile cosy cartel system. Tom shared his success with the West Australian community. He became the state's biggest philanthropist. He made major donations to many causes and charities. There was only one strict condition on his donations. He was to not be identified as the donor. As a result, his generosity was not widely known, neither was his story or what he had done for West Australians.

Tom however could not extend his success to the major eastern states.

The existing chains formed a cartel. They all discounted products in their stores to be less than Tom's prices, but only those within a close geographic location to Tom. They did not discount prices in all their other stores. This strategy succeeded in eliminating Tom's ability to generate profits and this successfully kept him from expanding into their markets.

At the height of his success in 1969 Tom had purchased the pastoral lease of Dirk Hartog Island. It is a mini paradise in the Indian Ocean of 630 square kilometres. His family still live on it. They originally managed the island's pastoral business. However, in 2006, the family returned the lease to the government in exchange for them establishing and giving the family four freehold properties on the island, totalling 100 acres and run this now as a tourist destination.

How Tom achieved his remarkable success is a great example of innovation and understanding organisations. Unfortunately, the demise of Tom's great company was undeservedly sad, and is a lesson in staying with a business you understand. In 1972 he went into investments in land, financed by a major loan taken out in Swiss Francs. In 1977, following major exchange rate moves, he defaulted on his loan, his company went into receivership and creditors finally got only 5 cents in the dollar. Tom and his wife, left virtually penniless, went to live on Dirk Hartog Island. Tom remained there as a recluse, living with his wife until his death in 1997, with his wife dying eight years later. You should have a more detailed look at Tom's life and his achievements. It is a little known, but remarkable story, of the rise and fall of one of Australia's largest retail empires, at one stage in fourth place nationally, and of a truly remarkable man and unsung hero. Tom's mistake, one frequently made, was venturing into a field where he had no experience.

I applied the stock turnover principle that Tom employed, in a national metals and engineering company in which, among other roles, I was inventory manager of a substantial multi-million-dollar inventory. I was not happy with the stock management computer algorithm the company was using. This led me to manage the old-fashioned way, using what Edward de Bono referred to as a teraflop neck-top computer, and at the same time draft a paper on Inventory Management in a Metals Marketing Environment. I sent this to the chair of the company board. As a result, they flew me interstate to address a full board meeting. At it I advised that while the IT department knew a lot about computers, they did not understand markets and supply chains. I knew little of computers but knew a lot about markets. The proof of this was in a doubling of stock turn rate under manual control and a 50% increase in gross profit, some millions of dollars. The IT problem had resulted from the IT tail wagging the dog. After the board meeting the dog started wagging the tail again. As a direct result inventory management, financial management and information management were all greatly improved. Another result was that I was offered a senior management job reporting directly to the board. For family reasons I declined this, to then be told that if I declined, I could say goodbye to my future. I did decline and did say goodbye, but on my terms.

Leaderless Groups

Wilfred Bion was a British psychoanalyst and founder member of the Tavistock Institute known for his work on group dynamics, including research on leaderless groups. In his research, Bion observed very interesting group behaviour by accident. He was to lead and help a group of PTSD war veterans. Arriving to meet the group, he was unsure of how to proceed and, while silently contemplating what to do, observed that the group started reacting to his lack of leadership. He went on to recognise that when groups lacked a designated leader or authority figure, they often exhibited fascinating behaviours and dynamics. One of his key concepts is the "Basic Assumption" group, where he identified three primary states:

Basic Assumption – dependency: In this state, group members may seek a leader or authority figure to provide direction and guidance. They then rely on this figure to take care of their needs and make decisions for them.

Basic Assumption – fight/flight: In this state, the group members might engage in conflict or avoid facing issues altogether. They may react with aggression or flee from the group's responsibilities.

Basic Assumption – pairing: This state involves the formation of intense, emotionally charged pairs within the group. Members may focus on interpersonal relationships and create an atmosphere of romanticised ideals but, at the same time, do some healing.

Bion's work highlighted the way leaderless groups could exhibit different, often irrational, behaviours as they struggle to cope with anxiety and uncertainty. However, if they developed and evolved well, they could have powerful healing qualities for participants. These insights have been valuable, not only in psychoanalysis but also in understanding group dynamics in various contexts, such as organisational behaviour and social psychology. In practice, using leaderless group concepts as a group development process is extraordinarily difficult. In the Tavistock Institute Group Exploratory Conference, most participants simply did not get it and what it entailed.

I will describe a case where I employed it, fortunately with great success.

The Nuns' Story

A senior member of the Catholic administration approached me to see if I was willing to undertake a consulting assignment in one of the larger orders of nuns. I said I would like to, and a three-day seminar workshop was arranged. This was to be conducted in one of the metropolitan Convents. I had been informed that the problem the order faced was one of communication. I have to say that every organisation, for whom I have done any consulting assignments have said that they have a communication problem. In over 90% of these cases, they do not have a communication problem. What they have is a communication symptom of a deeper problem. The challenge then is to try and find the cause, source or origin of the deeper problem.

I decided I would employ a leaderless group approach to this problem and just see what happened. It was a journey of discovery for all of us. The nuns had been advised that the object of the workshop was to resolve a communication problem, and I was their consultant to assist them.

The day arrived and I was taken to a large hall in which some 40+ nuns from all the different convents were sitting in a large circle. I had arranged for one seat to be left empty for me. I sat down in this, bowed my head, looked at the ground and said nothing and continued to look down, thus avoiding eye contact. There was absolute silence except for the scrape of a chair, but slowly, one could sense increasing tension and pressure build up. I knew and could feel the immense pressure that was being placed on me to fulfil the role expectations of the participants. I was surreptitiously sneaking a look at the group and could see them staring at me intently. I wondered whether I had made an error of judgement, and the nuns would just go into meditative states. However, this was not to be. Suddenly there was an explosion of breath from one nun who said, "I have to talk"; at the same time, she was looking around the group for someone to support her. Her action in Tavistock language was called the "plop"; the group then underwent a progressive process of pairing with participants looking for kindred spirits, with whom they could engage. Meanwhile I am still looking at the floor and making surreptitious observations.

With the tension broken and pairing happening, stories about the issues the different nuns were confronting in their convents started to be told, and the group norms about listening without interrupting, and taking turns allowing others to speak started developing. I was still looking at the floor. The morning tea break arrived. After this we returned to the plenary session. Like earlier, the group was developing nicely, and learning was taking place, and this took us to lunchtime. Our workshop was limited to three days. It can easily take longer for groups to get through norming and enter the performing stage, so I decided to intervene. After lunch, I handed out a questionnaire associated with the Johari window model. This is a window with four panes. One is "Known to self and known to others", the second is "Known to self but not known to others", the third is" Known to others but not known to self", and the fourth is "Not known to self and not known to others". The object of the exercise is to maximise, what is known to self and known to others, as a basis for openness leading to good interpersonal communication and relationships. The questionnaire asks questions over a wide range of topics. One section is about sex, asking questions such as who, was your favourite sexual partner, what are your favourite sexual activities and what are your most frequent sexual fantasies. I thought hard about this, but decided it was not my role to be censor. The participants had the freedom to respond or not. Having handed out the uncensored questionnaire I went to my chair and looked at the ground but was again surreptitiously observing what occurred. The nuns all started looking at one another and then one or two started completing the questionnaire; then everyone was doing it. When I saw that most people had completed it and were sitting back, I called a tea break. But before breaking I discussed how and why I had not assumed the mantle of censor.

In response to this, the Mother Superior replied, saying, "David, on behalf of myself and all my sisters here, I'd like to thank you for treating us like women and not the third sex. We are women and we have the same feelings and emotions as other women; like other women we have known sexual desires and thought about sexual experiences." At the tea break I was confronted by many of the nuns, smiling and offering me cakes and tea or coffee. This process, the outcome, and the comment of the Mother Superior had completely changed the cultural norms in the group. Suddenly, nothing was taboo. There was no need for self-censorship and the nuns all felt secure in opening-up and telling their peers about their true thoughts and feelings. These included feeling isolated, insecure, or inadequate; and they could now say this without fear of ridicule or criticism, knowing they would be listened to and supported. Very interestingly, I was now an accepted member the group, and no longer expected to be the leader, but rather an on-call consultant. Additionally, my gender seemed no longer relevant, given the nature of some topics and candid discussions.

This now became a group focussed on its members and their welfare. Smaller groups were formed to discuss special issues and report back in plenary sessions. In the process they discovered what the real problem was in their order. It was not communication. The real problem was that while they were caring for their flock, they were not caring for one another. In the group process they had found they could share their fears and perceived shortcomings, and that their peers, their sisters would not only really listen, but they would also try and help. It had become a healing group. This was an ideal outcome. At the conclusion of the three days the Mother Superior said, "David. We would all like to thank you. We did not get what we asked for, but you helped us find what we needed. This is the realisation of how important it is that we care for one another." I had just received one of the greatest compliments of my career.

Managing by Walking Around

The typical hierarchical organisational structure in most companies makes it almost impossible to get effective two-way vertical communication about what is happening at the coalface through to senior management and vice versa without major censorship and modification. Information from the bottom goes through, especially in bureaucratic structures, so many filters and individuals, who consciously or unconsciously modify the message, sometimes maliciously or to advantage themselves. This also happens with messages coming from senior management to the frontline or coalface. An illustration of this is the well-known military story, where a message passed from one person to another ended up with "Send reinforcements we are going to advance" becoming, "Send three and four pence we are going to a dance! One solution to this is senior management walking around to communicate directly with those at all levels in the enterprise as done by Robert Townsend in Avis.

Lord Marks of Broughton

A simple example of MBWA involved Simon Marks, who served as Chairman and President of Marks & Spencer, the famous British retail store. He played a key role in its modernisation and expansion through the 1960s and 1970s. His emphasis throughout was on quality and service. One day, while walking through one of their stores, he noted a young sales lady filling in forms, rather than attending to waiting customers that was her prime role. This small observation led him to commence a review of all paperwork being completed in the business to eliminate all unnecessary documents.

As a result, in the following year Marks and Spencer's reduced their paper consumption on documentation by more than 100 tonnes and this material cost was a fraction of the time and cost in completing and filing it. This non-essential form filling was time lost in productive income-earning sales or other activities. It illustrates how important it is to observe the many different things that are happening in an organisation and ask the question, "Why we are doing this, and could there be a better way?" It is also vital that you ask the right people how to do things better.

An Automobile Story and a Perceptive New Supervisor

I am reminded of a story a car-loving colleague told me. He had been in the United States and visiting a General Motors assembly plant, in which they assembled two of their leading brands on the same production line in different batches. The time taken to do a complete line change for the new vehicle run was typically 12 days. A new production supervisor had been made responsible for this line and decided to see if they could devise any improvements. In the past, engineers and production managers had dictated this process, but she decided to collaborate with the people on the production line. She did, and they developed a significantly different process. She took the developed process to senior management, and they asked her how much the processing time had improved. She replied, "Well, we have managed to get it down to eight". Senior management were amazed. "What? Down from twelve to eight days?" "No." she replied, "down to eight hours!" The downtime cost savings were enormous, as it amounted to an astonishing 10-20% potential increase in production time in a year. This is just one example of many I have known where amazing solutions to manufacturing or processing industries have been made by those who know best, and they are those engaged in the process.

On a much smaller scale, I had a similar experience in one company I worked with. I had noticed two filing clerks busy all day filing customer orders into customer files. I asked why we were doing this. It emerged that it was in case customers did not get their orders. Despite still not getting the logic behind this, I said that if a customer did not receive an order, we would get a phone call within hours. This practice was stopped and thenceforth orders were just filed in dated order files, a virtual saving of two staff roles. No orders were lost as a result!

The simple moral to these stories is, do not hesitate to question every activity undertaken and simply ask, "What would happen, what would we lose or what would we damage if we stopped doing this?" In a surprising number of cases the answer will be, "Nothing." We should periodically look at every activity and see if there are new ways or innovative technologies that will allow us to do it differently or more efficiently. This is increasingly so when the rate of change and emergence of new products, processes or technologies is exponential.

Beating the Bureaucracy

As mentioned before, the distortion and editing of information flowing up and down the formal structure is constant and extensive. Seldom will senior management have any detailed idea of what is happening at the coalface or front line, unless they get down there, and unless the culture allows or better still, promotes and encourages free and uncensored communication between management and staff. Even then it will always still be edited, filtered or miscommunicated in some way.

Getting the Truth.

There are alternative strategies that can be employed to have ongoing, direct access to the shop floor or front line. A famous and very successful manager, who realised the inefficiencies of the bureaucratic process, employed one. He established his own direct links, bypassing the bureaucracy, to the front line and shop floor. He was Konosuke Matsushita (1894-1989).

Matsushita was a Japanese industrialist and the founder of Panasonic Corporation. He was a prominent figure in the development of the Japanese electronics industry and a pioneer in creating innovative consumer products. His philosophy and principles make an excellent template or model for any organisation.

Konosuke Matsushita's life and contributions include:

In 1918, at the age of 23, he founded Matsushita Electric Industrial Co., Ltd., which later became Panasonic Corporation. He started the company by inventing, unbelievably, a better light socket! In Japan there were no wall sockets for electricity. So, Matsushita, recognising this, designed a light bulb socket insert with two outlets. One was for a lightbulb, and one was a power source for other electrical items. This revolutionised the use of electrical appliances in Japan. From this simple start, the company expanded to produce a vast range of electrical and electronic products.

He was known for his dedication to producing high-quality products. His famous philosophy was "not to produce a single product that is not first-rate." It was this commitment to quality that significantly contributed to the success and reputation of Panasonic.

He also developed a management philosophy known as the "Seven Principles of Management" These were akin to the seven principles of bushido in the lives of samurai warriors. The seven principles were the foundation of the culture that Matsushita desired for his corporation and the principles that continued to guide Panasonic's business practices.

They are principles that regrettably too few companies follow.

Let's look at the seven principles

Contribution to Society

We will follow the Basic Management Objective for society's benefit.

Fairness and Honesty

We will be fair and honest in all our business dealings and personal conduct.

Cooperation and Team Spirit

We will combine our abilities to accomplish our shared goals together and value team spirit.

Untiring Effort for Improvement

We will try to improve our business's ability to contribute to society.

Courtesy and Humility

We will always be cordial and modest, and respect others for good social relationships.

Adaptability

We will continually adapt our thinking and behaviour to meet the ever-changing conditions around us.

Gratitude

We will act out of a sense of gratitude for all the benefits we have received.

Matsushita believed that businesses had a responsibility to contribute to the betterment of society. He was a strong advocate for corporate social responsibility and philanthropy. As with some other innovators and great corporate leaders his legacy extends well beyond his role as an entrepreneur; he is frequently cited as one of the pioneers of the modern Japanese business system, and his principles of management and innovation have inspired business leaders around the world. It would be truly great to see national statements of corporate principles like those of Matsushita. With those principles in place, to then see corporate performance evaluated against them, in addition to evaluation against financial regulations, and profit performance. It could well result in highly desirable cultural change.

Monopolies and getting around legislated Change

AT&T

AT&T held a near-monopoly on telephone service in the United States for most of the 20th century. In 1913, the U.S. Department of Justice filed an antitrust lawsuit against the company, leading to a settlement in 1914 known as the Kingsbury Commitment. This settlement allowed AT&T to continue its monopoly but with certain government regulations. In 1984, 70 years later, after another antitrust action, AT&T was broken up into several regional "Baby Bell" companies, with names like Verizon, CenturyLink, and BellSouth. AT&T retained its long-distance services and began to diversify into other areas.

In the late 1990s and early 2000s, AT&T re-entered the local telephone market by re-acquiring some of the Baby Bell companies. It also expanded its services to include wireless, internet, and cable TV. Then in 2015, AT&T acquired DirecTV, a satellite television provider, and later purchased Time Warner, a major media conglomerate, in 2018. These moves transformed AT&T into a major player in the media and entertainment industry. It rebranded its media assets as Warner Media and launched the streaming service HBO Max, which offers a wide range of content, including HBO's original programming. AT&T has continued to change and evolve, with an increased focus on expanding its telecommunications and media offerings.

In 2023 AT&T is the world's largest telecommunications company, providing voice coverage in 220 countries and data in 190 countries and is the largest provider of fixed and mobile telephones services in the United States. It is 13th in the Fortune 500 and has revenue of 120 billion dollars. So, following the Department of Justice antitrust actions starting over 100 years ago AT&T, did divest but then simply reinvested acquiring new companies and diversifying. So, in subsequent years while no longer a monopoly it has still managed to successfully dominate in its field within the USA and globally.

Standard Oil: The Seven Sisters

It is instructive to compare AT&T to another massive corporation, which behaved in an analogous way when confronted by the regulatory forces of the United States Justice system.

Standard Oil was not just the largest in its field it was the largest corporation in the world. Under the leadership of John D. Rockefeller, the world's first billionaire, through merger and acquisition of many other companies, it gained effective monopoly control of all the production, refining, transport, and distribution of oil in the United States. Rockefeller let the other myriad companies take all the risks in exploring and wildcatting oil discoveries. He had recognised that the virtually risk-free and critical central role in the oil industry was in refining and distribution. His control and tentacles had spread far beyond the United States; I once read that at one point he controlled over 80% of the world distribution of oil.

In 1911, the United States Justice Department went into trust busting mode. The Standard Oil monopoly was dismantled, and, in the process, it spawned more than 40 subsidiary companies. The principal ones among them were seven oil companies that included Exxon, Mobil, Chevron, Gulf Oil, Texaco BP and Shell. They became individually the seven largest corporations in the world. They were called the seven sisters as, unlike brothers who tend to fight and compete, sisters cooperate, and they did and have done so, publicly, or privately for over 100 years.

So, when we seek to understand organisations, it is evident that, as with individuals and societies, self-preservation in the face of an external threat, is a powerful motive that can lead to different forms of resistance or subversive action. In the case of both corporations, they complied with the structural demands of the Justice Department, but at the same time ensured that things continued much as they had before, just less overtly, by maintaining close family relationships and communications within and between their now disseminated enterprises.

Industry dominance is a major issue in Australia. The land of monopolistic or oligopolistic markets. We have industry domination by a few companies in retail, food, timber and hardware, electronics, office supplies, garden plants, and liquor. Apart from retail we have oligopoly markets in banking and finance, wireless telecoms, insurance, and consulting. It is unclear whether this market situation is bad or good for Australian consumers. There are good economic arguments that can be put for both sides. There does seem however to be more questions on the power of retailers to, particularly in relation to farm produce. They take a hard line in the supply chain, forcing prices down so that farmers have difficulty surviving with such low profits. There comes a time when governments need to intervene in monopoly behaviour and protect farmers or similar businesses in the supply chain. There is pressure for the Australian government to do this and avoid loss of local production, as food independence and self-sufficiency is a vital national priority. In many countries, farmers are assisted with farm subsidies. In the EU and United States these exceed sixty billion dollar a year.

Understanding Criminal influences on Organisations

The extent to which criminals and criminal groups can influence organisational behaviour is largely unrecognised by the general law-abiding public. This influence can be found in the most unlikely markets, so let's look at some examples.

Milk in Australia was a price-controlled product until the governing bodies were wound up in 2000; I had been asked by a state government to investigate and see if a proposed price increase sought by the dairy processing industry was justified.

In my forensic accountant's role, it did not take long to see that both major companies were stacking the cost of milk production, with many of the costs being incurred in their other dairy products, such as ice creams, yoghurts etc. However, there were two other puzzling features. One was the reluctance of management to hold discussions with me, and the other was that nowhere could I find where or how, the total volume of milk flowing through the processing companies, was being accurately monitored.

After a full day of investigation, I was at home when I received a call from a milk distributor that I had met. He asked me if I would meet him confidentially at a tavern where he could provide some useful information. It turned out that the truck drivers transporting all the milk were very much in control of the industry. Unless distributors agreed to take a percentage of "hot milk", milk that was being stolen in transit and from the processors, then the distributors got no deliveries. I sat down and worked out the value of how much milk was being stolen. Daily it was, other than drugs, possibly the biggest criminal enterprise in the state. Who would have thought that milk, of all things, would be a criminal target? An outcome of this was that the desired milk price increase was greatly reduced, along with a requirement that milk processing volumes be accurately measured and audited. This and the total change of milk distribution, to be primarily through supermarkets, sounded the death knoll of the old milk distributors and the "hot milk" industry.

Other examples with which I am familiar include two stock-exchange listed mining companies. One was doing exploration work in Russia with a Russian partner. Having expended some $40 million, and proven there was a significant ore reserve, the company sent a senior executive to Russia to finalise the mine development plans. On arriving, and meeting the Russian partner, they were told that they had a choice. Leave the meeting by the stairs after they had signed the project over to the Russians, or by the window if they declined. This method of departure is not uncommon in Russia. Of course, the Russians acquired the project.

For another company working in Italy, it was simply the Mafia, in the guise of another company, advising the directors that the company would face ongoing problems unless they were willing to cede control to a new major shareholder. The Mafia were not looking at mining profits, but saw great opportunities to get significant inputs of government development funds, which they could then divert to other uses at their sole discretion.

The most publicised criminal groups in Australia are the so-called outlaw motorcycle gangs. They have their fingers in many pies, notably drug distribution Australia-wide, as well as chop shops selling illegal tobacco, tattoo parlours and sex related activities. A business friend told me that at one stage he had recourse to use their finance arm. It was like conventional finance companies with higher rates. However, you also had to accept more risk along with serious repercussions if repayment commitments were not met!

One Way of Dealing with Criminal Threats (Not Advocated!)

Back to my good friend John. He had got contracts with most major hospitals in NSW to install his electrolysis machines and purchase their film at agreed market rates for silver. With this achieved, he decided to expand his operations to the adjacent state of Victoria and went down to call on some major hospitals. This set the cat among the pigeons. One of the well-known family gangs in Melbourne had got into the market and were purchasing film at very low prices and making easy profits. They did not have the electrolysis machines for fixer that John had designed and manufactured. However, they were determined that the interloper from Sydney was not going to operate on their turf. To this end, they put a contract on John They also sent his wife wreaths and "In Memoriam" cards. In addition, someone had broken into the family home, leaving a trail of damage, and a threatening message frightening his family.

John held discussions with Victorian police, but the upshot was that these were just threats, and they could do little. A week or so later, I was with John and his business partner, another good friend, when he asked John what was happening about Melbourne and the contract. "Oh! That is all resolved," said John. "I should have told you! I have put a contract from Sydney on the guys in Melbourne. If I go, they go so it is checkmate." On this news his partner resigned from the business that day! And thus, it was indeed checkmate. John expanded down to Victoria to all the major hospitals without incident. However, from then on, he always travelled with weapons in his car, a shotgun and sidearm. This is another illustration that solutions to organisational problems can be not so much of what you know, as who you know, especially when the solutions to the problems are found outside the organisation.

Searching for the Real Source of Organisation problems

The Finance Company Problem

I must preface this story by stating that, for many years, I planned to write a thesis on the interaction between family and organisational life. This was because I had seen some fascinating examples of this and little research in the field. But as John Lennon once said, "life is what happens while you are making plans". We would all be familiar with or know of examples where the stresses, setbacks or problems faced in the workplace are taken home, often with adverse effects on the family and family relationships. These can range from simple expressed frustrations, escape into alcohol, or more abusive outcomes for spouses and children. A quite simple reason for this is that the home is a safe environment, where one can vent and exhibit behaviours, behaviours that would almost certainly result in being sacked if exhibited in the workplace. What is rarely recognised, in fact I have never seen any references to it in any sociology or psychology text that I have read, is the converse, whereby circumstances and situations in the home environment can lead to good, but sometimes seriously adverse behaviours in the organisation. We have previously looked at how psychopaths can and do disrupt organisations to satisfy personal cravings and needs that are effectively home sourced. This is not about psychopaths. It is a different pathology, and this is an example.

At the risk of being repetitive, I have to say again that, when looking for the source of problems, you need to look both inside and outside of the organisation. You need to look with eyes wide open and be willing to examine potential sources that seem outlandish or are even outside your contractual remit or charter.

I was once asked by a major bank if I would undertake an assignment in a large and highly successful finance company that they had acquired. The finance company was doing very well but the concern was that the staff turnover rate was extremely high, and they had lost some very talented staff. The previous owner still managed the company. This had been part of the acquisition contract. I was to go in to technically check the financial and accounting structure, as I was qualified in those fields.

However, the real objective was to find out why staff were leaving in droves. I met the managing director and was given carte blanche to investigate whatever I wanted. It took no time at all to discover that the cause of the staff turnover was the behaviour of the managing director. He would go around with a little thundercloud over his head, being hypercritical of how things were being done. He was castigating staff in front of their peers. He did not have a good word to say for anyone or anything. In short, he was creating a work environment in which no one felt respected, where no one was happy, and where everyone was under the constant threat of criticism or worse. I was trying to understand or get a handle on why he was always behaving like this and was getting nowhere. I suddenly thought, "Let's try a different approach," so I asked staff whether there were any times when he was not like it. Surprisingly, they said there were.

So, the search now turned to why was this so? After more discussions and further probing, it turned out that these occasions were when his wife went on holidays. This required, if I was to understand why, a quantum leap into investigating the home life of the MD. This was not in my remit and did raise some ethical questions: "Could I? and Should I?", as without doing so I was not going to get to the source of the problem, I decided that I would.

What I discovered was that our MD had come from a working-class background, had been educated at a state and not public school, and had not gone to university. He had started his business in a small way, grown it quite fast, as he was very astute and streetwise, until it was a substantial company, and he was quite wealthy. Along the way, he had met and married a young woman from a wealthy suburb. She had professional parents and a private school education. They had children, but his wife soured their relationship by constantly putting him down, seeing him as a misfit in her society, and electing to have her holidays with "her type of friends". All this criticism, the negativity, and the burden she placed on him daily, went away with her on her holidays and he was free to be himself, a nice friendly and outgoing person. The one who had built the company from scratch.

My problem now was how the hell am I going confront him and deal with this, as I'd effectively been a spy and breached his trust. There was only one way. I asked for an appointment to meet him late morning. I went into his office, sat down when invited, and said that I had a confession to make. I told him I had not been sent to check on accounting and finance, but on high staff turnover, and had discovered that he was the cause. I said that furthermore, I had discovered why he was the cause. I explained this had required me to investigate him, his family life and the role of his wife.

He exploded; for a moment I thought we might have a physical altercation. I then said, "I want to tell you that your wife is making you kill your baby, and she is being successful!" He said nothing and I said nothing, and just sat there and waited. Time stops in these circumstances. He suddenly spoke and said, "I had no idea, but on thinking about what you have said you are absolutely right." (He used a few more expletives in his version). He said, "I can now see how my wife was goading and manipulating me. There will be no more manipulation. I promise you I will look after my baby and ensure its future as a successful adult. Thank you, David, for what you have shown me and for your honesty." We parted on that note. The outcome was that staff turnover dropped to nominal figures, and the whole climate and culture became a positive one. It would have been extremely interesting to see what subsequently occurred with his family. Let us compare this example to that of employees taking their problems home and venting because home is a safe environment. In the case of the MD, it was not his home but his organisation that was the safe environment, where he was able to vent and exhibit behaviours he could not display at home and allow his wife a further opportunity to confirm his social deficiencies. I have found many other examples where organisational problems have similar or related sources outside the organisation. It could be worthwhile reflecting on your own behaviours. Just arriving at work grumpy, edgy, or withdrawn elicits responses from colleagues, and those with whom you interact. These may be overt or covert and influence perceptions and behaviour of work colleagues. You have no doubt experienced this as both actor and audience. As I said earlier, it is an aspect of understanding organisations that would be rich to research, from both the psychology and sociology implications.

Government and Government Organisations

It is impossible to take a journey on understanding organisations without looking at government. When we look at the three tiers of government it is clearly the largest conglomerate organisation in Australia. While it has decreased in percentage terms over recent years, it still represents some 38% of gross domestic product in Australia. This is like the USA. By comparison in France it is 58% and in India 28%.

Governments principally differ from private enterprise in that their goals and objectives are normally deemed to be guided by what is called the triple bottom line TBL. There is a deemed TBL for socially responsible private sector companies namely, profits, people, and the planet. For government it is a little different. The idea is that government policies should have positive social, economic and environmental outcomes. These are frequently difficult to reconcile.

Government is also different from the private sector, in that the responsibility for the day-to-day functioning and achievement of goals is the responsibility of the bureaucrats in the relevant departments. In turn, they are subject to the whims of their masters, who are the politicians. The latter may well have personal objectives, typically such as being re-elected, that see them place demands on their bureaucracy, that are in total conflict with actions to improve things across the electorate. We are all familiar with the many phrases associated with politicians. Pork barrelling, nepotism, party politics, branch stacking, expense cheating, non-declaration of assets, conflicts of interest, and jobs for the boys, or girls. The clash between the politicians and the bureaucrats was beautifully parodied in those masterpieces of British TV, *Yes, Minister* and *Yes, Prime Minister.*

I had my own delightful experience of this. I was once invited to Canberra to join a panel that was advising the then Minister for Education and Training on tertiary training, with the focus on trade skills and tertiary but non-university education. This was due to my having headed up a national project developing management competencies for Australia and training courses for each of the competencies. TAFE was the primary national provider for trade skills and programs not taught at university, though private schools and colleges had also entered the field. The focus was on Competency Based Training, which was flavour of the month and the latest thing in the United Kingdom.

The panel was highbrow, with university professors and senior trade and industry people. I am certain I was the only member who had lectured and tutored in Universities and TAFE colleges. I disagreed with much of the change being proposed or recommended but my voice was drowned out by the heavyweights. I did have one opportunity to speak directly with the Minister. I told him about my reservations. But it was evident he knew little of the implications of the educational changes proposed. As a result, he could be misinformed and misdirected without recognising how or why. The main reason was, like other ministers, he had his swathe of advisors, and he only got to hear what they wanted to tell him. They heavily modified everything to suit their own agendas. In short, this is the same problems private sector executives face in getting unfiltered communications from the front line. Without this, managers can make some bewildering decisions. So it is with government, but often on a larger scale. This does help explain, otherwise inexplicable decisions made by ministers. I had agreed in my short face-to-face with the minister to submit a written report on what I felt could be useful and effective policies.

I do have to first recount my introduction to "Club Fed", as it was colloquially called. I was collected by a Commonwealth car at my home and driven to the airport, where I collected my business class tickets and entered the lounge. On arrival in Canberra, I was collected at the airport, driven to my extremely nice hotel to freshen up, and then my driver took me to the meeting room in Parliament House. I must admit I felt I could easily learn to enjoy being treated in this fashion as an important VIP. However, I also realised how a lifestyle like this would seriously shield you from the realities outside Club Fed.

Subsequently, leaving Canberra after our meetings I arrived home, driven again in my chauffeured Commonwealth car, but my little adventure was not yet over.

On arriving home, I duly drafted my report and submitted it to the secretary of the Department, effectively the top bureaucrat. A couple of weeks had elapsed when I received a phone call from the secretary. "Good morning, David, Roger here, I have been reading your report. It is an exceptionally good report, but I have a few problems with it. You have said we should undertake a considerable number of actions and make commitments", and these were his actual words "could I ask you to vague it up a bit?". "Could you change your words to include others such as 'could', 'may', 'subject to', 'following investigation', 'assess', 'potentially', and 'appraise' in order that we won't be as committed to action". I smiled at the time, and declined to make the changes, saying I am afraid Roger that someone else will need to vague it up!

My first encounter with government was when I was a new commerce graduate. A family friend said the government needed people like me, so I joined a department titled Industrial Development. It turned out that this department exclusively monitored and annually audited, some forty-seven companies that had received government-backed loans from a major bank. The loans were to fund the ventures they had brought to the department.

The department was staffed by clerical staff and accountants who reported to the chief accountant. However, none of these accountants were qualified accountants. They were bureaucratic titles, and their knowledge of accounting and finance was negligible. I was given the job of reviewing these companies and submitting a report on them. This I was told, should keep me occupied for three to six months. I started on them straight away, and at the end of the day took a bundle home to work on them there. I was fascinated by the diversity of projects funded, and even more by how they had ever got approval for funding. By the end of a week, I had looked at and analysed every company and, to put it bluntly, many were quite simply scams. Moreover, all of them, especially the scams, were either effectively insolvent or doomed to fail. Only one company had any prospect of being successful and growing. In the process of examining them, it suddenly occurred to me that with all the major projects creating financial problems, one accounting company had submitted the proposals. I will briefly give two examples.

The Dairy Farm

This was located over 2000 kilometres north of traditional dairy country in a hot semi-arid region of Western Australia. It had been funded for some years and seemed to just be keeping its head above water. However, when I looked at the accounts there was a glaring and major income omission. I took it to the senior accountant, Alan, as it was one of his clients, and asked him to review the accounts. This he did and said that they all looked good. I asked him why the cows were producing milk, to which he replied, "Because they are milking cows." I then advised Alan that a prerequisite to cows providing milk was that they had a calf, and that the calves were taken from them so the milk could be extracted in a dairy.

Alan was a city boy who knew nothing about dairies and in addition was not a qualified accountant who knew what to look for. Despite the farm having been operating for over five years there were no records of any income from calves. There should have been about 250 calves, yet there was no increase in herd numbers. I investigated further and found that we were funding the establishment of his son's dairy farm 2000 kilometres south, including his costs of feed, veterinary costs and so on. These fees were all charged to the northern dairy. His son's dairy, with minimal costs, was doing extremely well! Our support was terminated, but nothing further was done as if charges had been laid it could have proven very embarrassing.

The CB Hotel

This project involved the funding of a new hotel in a remote but beautiful part of the West Australian north-west coast. It was a major project requiring funds of well over a million dollars. This was an exceptionally large sum at the time. When I examined it, this project was in serious trouble. The original loan had been used up, and another major loan approved to complete construction, but this additional loan was already looking inadequate to complete the project. It was evident that the second loan had been a political imperative. A failure of a project of this magnitude would have been political dynamite. My analysis raised two serious questions: "How the hell was this approved in the first place?" And second, "How did the funds for construction get spent so fast?" The answer to the first question was easily answered. The original project proposal, submitted by this suspect firm of accountants, was based on fantasy cashflow forecasts. Income as well as operating costs were based on unreal and impossible assumptions.

Just a couple of points illustrate this. The income had been based on 90% occupancy of every available room for 365 days a year. This is unheard of. On the cost side there had been no provision for staff accommodation of any kind. This would obviously have significantly reduced rooms available for guests. So, the assumption was presumably that staff would be sleeping in tents on the beach. In addition, there was nothing about the cost of providing power, or the copious amounts of water that would be required by guests, staff and operations. This latter, for example, had to be sourced from a distant aquifer, and treated to be potable. Briefly, the project projections were based on totally unrealistic income and cost assumptions. With any professional scrutiny, this should have been picked up immediately and the project rejected.

The second question was more difficult to answer and required a lot more delving into the costs incurred in the project. This soon showed the influence of the same accounting company. It turned out that companies associated with them, were the providers of construction and trade services, as well as all furnishings, facilities and equipment used throughout the building. In every case the hourly rates and equipment costs were far higher than costs in other comparable projects. The project was being bled dry by its suppliers. Tighter controls, competitive tenders and project supervision brought costs under control, and the project was eventually completed, admittedly at nearly triple the initial cost estimates. It is, years later, a major tourist destination.

Having completed the analysis of every company and found that none had real prospects, apart from the hotel, I recommended that none should receive further funding. My review and recommendations were as follows:

1.   The project selection and auditing processes were clearly a failure. Statistically, had the funds available been allocated on a random unaudited basis by picking numbers from a barrel, the probability of success would have been no worse.

2.   The staff cost of the annual investigating, auditing and administration of the department, and its rent, significantly exceeded the total value of the funds being administered. In addition, it had failed to be effective.

3. There was not one real success story among all the companies funded under The Industries Act; all of them were moribund.
4. Advances made under the act should be immediately ceased and the Industries Act terminated.

All four recommendations were implemented, but it illustrates how well-intended legislation can be easily abused, with funds redirected or wasted when the resources could have been applied to more needful and socially desirable projects.

From memory it was Australian Prime Minister, Paul Keating who said, "Never get between a State Premier and a bag full of money"! The same behaviours are evident every time governments make funds available for economic or social programmes. With these programmes we find that individuals and companies, with little or no moral compass or integrity, arrive like vultures around carrion, intent on picking the programmes clean of funds.

Governments, but especially the Federal Government, are constantly coming out with policies to support employment, training and education, childcare, social care for the elderly, disability care, industries, innovation, and social equality, just to name a few. The annual sums allocated to these areas in Australia are more than $200 billion. I have followed some of these programs over the years, and I can say with an over 90% probability of being correct, that virtually every single one has been ruthlessly exploited.

Large, listed companies have done this as have a host of small businesses. Many of these latter having been established with the sole purpose of getting access to the billions of dollars the government would be handing out. Their objective is to simply divert the dollars into their own coffers. In this way, billions have been stolen, and are still being stolen.

The funds, as a result, frequently end up in the hands of unscrupulous people. They easily find numerous ways to divert funds into their hands. They use offshore entities, insolvency, complex company structures, phoenixing and other similar strategies, all enabling them to keep their snouts in the money trough. These are the rogue operators, who have drained and still drain, funds from the honest and genuine companies attempting to apply the funds to the purposes for which they had been created.

There have been times when I have written to different government departments, describing how funds were being misappropriated, but I have only ever received one response. I will mention a very simple one. This was an early business migration program where, if you came with $500,000 and invested it in a company, you were a contender for citizenship. This was poorly monitored and, when I investigated it, I could not find any successful operating businesses that existed, despite the number of people who had entered under the program. On further investigation, it turned out that applicant one brought in their $500,000, purchased a shelf company and a registered business name at a cost of about $500 and deposited their funds in it. So, they had met the basic requirements. The almost $500k was then sent offshore and applicant two followed the same strategy. It was a $500k merry-go-round. I contacted the department, told them what I had found, and said there was a simple solution; they could get the taxation department to monitor the shelf company accounts. The response was, "We couldn't do that as it would be an invasion of privacy." Unbelievable! As they constantly and freely invade every Australian citizen's privacy!

Fortunately, such programs now require applicants to meet a complete range of criteria. Another example I recall was the government offering a $6,000 interest-free loan to help young unemployed people get into training and work. What happened in this case was many doctors, lawyers, accountants, and other professionals, who had their sons and daughters as employees in their family trusts to reduce taxation, instantly sacked their children. They were then unemployed, and they immediately applied for the loans. It is doubtful if any of the genuine unemployed, for whom the loans were designed got a look in. A student in one of my business classes was a recipient of such a loan! His desperate need was epitomised by his secretary. She drove onto campus in an iridescent green Porsche 911, sat in the lecture theatre, took shorthand and recorded notes. She then drove off in the Porsche to give them to her "unemployed" loan recipient.

The number and extent of scams in employment, and in post-secondary trade training have probably been among the worst cases of misappropriation and theft in recent years. It has resulted in major losses of many millions of government dollars. There has also been great losses and distress caused to thousands of migrants and overseas students, loss of trust in our employment and training establishments, and even some diplomatic issues. In every case, where the government is handing out money, it rarely has effective systems in place to ensure its funds go to genuine enterprises, or to ensure programs aren't being exploited. There are frequently major deficiencies or holes in the legislation or administration that the scammers find and use. They then run riot, mercilessly exploiting the government and innocent victims. With education and training, the victims had been seduced to enrol with claims of attractive employment or citizenship opportunities. These were being made by unscrupulous highly questionable employment services and training companies without adequate government scrutiny.

It was a truly sad day when the government decided that employment services and post-secondary and trade education would be privatised, naively thinking the private sector providers would all operate with honesty and integrity. It makes you wonder what planet our politicians live on, or is it an outcome of living in Club Fed? In another area of government decision making, we should look for better ways in which politicians can be prevented from decision making that can result in personal gain. This has been evident on both sides of politics. How often do we see politicians well rewarded for legislative decisions they have supported, with subsequent lucrative employment in the related private sector.

How to develop and successfully implement fantastic policies!

The suggestion that I have put to government policymakers is incredibly simple. When you have any policy proposal that involves handing out bags of money, especially but not exclusively when those getting access to the money are private sector individuals or companies, you should first do one thing. Get together a panel of the shrewdest, most cunning, dishonest, crafty, deceitful, unscrupulous, duplicitous, unprincipled, and unethical lawyers, accountants, not forgetting the big four, and businessmen. Once you have assembled them, tell them they will get paid very generously for every way that they can find to exploit the legislation. Only after this step has been taken, and legislation amended to eliminate all known avenues for exploitation, should the legislation be enacted. Had governments of every persuasion done this, many billions of dollars would have been saved annually, plus the legislation would have achieved its purpose and objectives more successfully.

Messianic Leaders

This is a special category of leaders. There have been many messianic leaders in religious, extremist, and cult organisations.

There have been examples, many and most publicised ones in the United States. These have been companies promising amazing things, only to eventually crash and burn, some of which have even led to executives being jailed. These include Enron, Blockbuster, Allied Crude, DeLorean, and Theranos, just to name a few. The lesson here is that you should beware of messiahs, whatever the context. They can of course be a force for good. Steve Jobs in Apple would be one while Oprah Winfrey would be one as a television presenter. The organisational lesson we can learn from looking at messianic leaders and history is simple. Get behind the rhetoric and focus only on facts, serious research, and the views of experienced investors or analysts, especially in this age of disruptor companies, capable of killing other companies virtually overnight. I can speak from experience having lost substantial sums of money from following an individual rather than the facts!

The Engineering Company and on Becoming a Messiah

I have left this story until last. It was the most fascinating consulting assignment I was ever engaged in. It illustrates the extent to which an organisation's behaviour can be the outcome of complex, undisclosed or hidden relationships. I must seriously abbreviate my account of this, as what occurred and what was learned took well over six months and thirty thousand words.

The company was based in London with its offices in Mayfair. It was an engineering business, with over 100+ engineers and surveyors and support staff employed. All were associated with the oil industry. The professional staff were being sent to the North Sea and the Gulf of Mexico, but primarily to the Middle East. This was due to the major client being Aramco. Aramco is the largest oil company in the world. In 2021, its net operating profit was over $160 billion and net cash flow over $185 billion. We even had a member of the Saudi royal family on our staff. He was a qualified structural engineer but was undertaking an additional degree course in chemical engineering. His reason was not a need for further education. It was that when he went home, he had four selected wives waiting for him to marry them. He was having so fantastic a time in London he had no desire to return home to be wed! This is not hard to understand. His allowance from the family oil income was 50,000 barrels a year, with an oil price of $US 39! This amounted to two million pounds a year, while the average workers income at the time in England was around fifteen thousand pounds a year! You could even buy a stately home for around one hundred thousand pounds. One of the Aramco managers did. I was asked to arrange an itinerary of stately home visits, collect him in a chauffeured Rolls Royce at the airport and drive him around to inspect them. I did this and he decided he would purchase the third property we visited. This was a beautiful Manor House on 50 acres in Berkshire 27 miles from the airport. England was in dire straits at the time and property prices were rock bottom and properties outside London were difficult to sell. The price of this home was 140,000 pounds. Our Aramco manager opened his case and said "there is 125,000 pounds cash here. Will you accept this"? The owner looked at his wife, she nodded, and he said "yes"! The case was full of black money. This was rampant in the oil industry then. In two other oil related projects I was involved with in the naughties it was still rampant.

I met the two joint managing directors of the company. One, let's say Rick, was the founder, sole owner and managing director. Rick had appointed Dave, an engineer as co-managing director. On the surface this seemed fine. Having been given the go-ahead, I started looking at the financial state of the company as a first step. I quickly realised that the company was technically insolvent with a large income but larger expenses. I also discovered that 90% of the income was from Aramco. This was a highly dangerous situation.

Rick the entrepreneur was a fascinating person, possibly bipolar. His moods could change fast and quite dramatically. When he was happy, he could be great fun and engage in outrageous actions. For example, one morning he arrived in a classic blue striped chemise, and a French beret, sporting a painted-on moustache and smoking a Gauloise cigarette, with a baguette in one hand. On other mornings, suffused with anger or with a bad hangover, he would literally walk through the office sweeping everything off desks that he passed. Staff always arrived well before the day's start time in order not to miss his latest behavioural outburst. Despite, or because of this, he was universally liked, being generous to a fault and totally unpredictable. Dave, the engineer, was the exact opposite, exhibiting behaviours somewhat like a sociopath. He killed any conversation in the office, and, even when staff met down at the local pub, conversation stopped when he walked in. He was socially reclusive, and had no friends in the company, except for Rick. I arranged to meet both directors in their homes to get a better feel of what they were like socially.

When I arrived at Dave's apartment it was all in shades of grey, with minimalist Scandinavian style furniture and there was sepulchral music playing. I literally felt that I was walking into a tomb or crypt. I wanted to get out as soon as possible but Dave wanted to talk. In the process, while talking about girlfriends, he told me he only went out with and had sex with women who could not speak English, so that he didn't have to have a conversation. Finally, after one drink I got out with the realisation that Dave had real issues.

Two days later my evening was with Rick. He had knocked two terraced houses together in Hammersmith. As soon as I walked in, the contrast to Dave's apartment could not have been starker. It was vibrant with colour, lovely furnishings and tapestries and paintings on the walls, the principal one being of a beautiful nude woman that was over two metres high. I immediately felt that this was the apartment of a gay person, as it was so reminiscent of apartments or homes of my gay friends in Sydney.

The dramatic difference between Rick and Dave told me that I had to do some serious thinking, given what I'd discovered. This was a situation unlike any I'd previously encountered. I checked with a couple of our female employees, who both said Rick showed no interest in them at all, and they had thought he could quite possibly be gay. This was even though he was overtly hetero in speech and manner at work, and a big rowdy follower of Rugby. We had a major parking station opposite us, that our offices overlooked. Rick regularly got his staff to go and chat to women waiting to go into it, saying their boss would enjoy having lunch or dinner with them. If any accepted he would wine and dine them.

Now, to the summary outcome of the initial analysis. This was after some weeks delving forensically into accounts, meeting professional staff, looking at operations and administration, and spending more time with Rick and Dave. I concluded that Dave had been appointed as co-director and senior engineer because Rick was in love with him, but had to keep this hidden. Dave was a disaster as a managing director. He had no idea how to manage, and absolutely no knowledge of accounting or finance. As a result, he had done nothing constructive for the company. It was floundering, and he was clearly responsible for the dire straits and insolvent state the company was now in, but Rick couldn't bring himself to fire him.

I could see that unless something dramatic was done the company would fail. Neither Dave nor Rick was capable of what was required, so I elected myself as de facto managing director. I'd met and become friends with most of the staff who were ready and willing to work with me. I organised a major advertising blitz, by phone, as we couldn't afford media. This was to promote our capabilities to the major oil and gas companies. We got a surprisingly good response. Over twenty-five executives representing eleven companies accepted an invitation to come to our office for an industry meeting three weeks away. On the day of the meeting, I took a company credit card and went shopping by taxi, with two staff members to upmarket shops. I bought whole smoked salmon, legs of ham, roasts of beef, lamb and chicken, plus a whole range of different breads, salads items, avocados, chutneys, cheeses, condiments, fruits and wickerwork baskets. I finished by purchasing all the alcohol including a good range of wines, spirits and beers, and hired all the glassware and trestle tables from the suppliers. Then, with the help of our staff, got this all laid out on the trestle tables. It looked great and sumptuous in something of a medieval banquet fashion!

I then got in touch with our recruitment company and rented a crowd of some 20 males and females. They were to be in the office when the guests were there, filing stuff in cabinets, sitting at computers, and making and receiving telephone calls between themselves! When guests arrived, it was a hive of activity. Our guests mingled with our engineers and surveyors, who I had coached on what to say and discuss. I excluded Rick and Dave from our presentation as their behaviour would have been unpredictable and risky, and their attendance was unnecessary. Our guests were suitably impressed by everything and were asking whether we were not too busy to handle their work. Naturally we convinced them that we could, as we had many staff away on overseas projects, and additional staff resources available that we could call on. The event was a great success!

We got over £1million of work on that afternoon alone, with promises of a lot more to come. In another financial restructuring relating to a major cost, I saved well over a million pounds a year and was additionally able to increase payments to staff without cost to the company. Two days later, a large group of staff invited me to the pub. I got there and they said they were all ready to leave the company and start a new company with me at the helm. I couldn't do it, not simply for ethical reasons, but it would not have worked for my family. Instead, I said I was confident, in the time I could spend there, that we would be able to ensure the company would continue to grow, and to make good profits. Its culture needed to be and would be quite different, and it should be a very good and fun place to work. In addition, to achieve the necessary culture change I would persuade Rick that Dave needed to go.

There were two important things that had happened over this time I'd spent with the company. Firstly, I was being treated like the Messiah, with all the engineers and surveyors being my disciples or followers. I had shown them they could have a much more secure, fun, enjoyable and profitable work environment. In short, every follower could go forward to a better future in a new culture.

Secondly Rick had recognised Dave had nearly destroyed his company.

Not only this, but he had now fallen in love with me. I had not only saved his company from insolvency, but it was now becoming very profitable. Apart from this Rick and I got on very well. When at his home after our marketing night I'd asked him whether he was gay, as his home reminded me of those of my gay friends. He initially looked angry and as though he was going to deny it, until I quickly said he didn't have to answer as it wouldn't affect our friendship.

This was when he offered me the earth to stay on as managing director. But I told him he had to sack Dave, as Dave was Death, and could only destroy the company. Plus, he had an excellent manager in one of the other engineers. This was Geoff, the engineer who had orchestrated the offer of mass resignations, to work in the new company headed by me. Dave was let go and Geoff took over as chief engineer. The company went on to become highly successful, with many corporate clients, not just Aramco. Later, it was taken over by an American multinational, earning Rick a truly handsome multimillion pound profit.

This story has been drastically edited to discuss only the final outcomes of my analysis not the many days, weeks and months involved in behavioural research and the process of analysis. Several of the findings, for example, were recommended as worthy papers for the Journal of Abnormal Psychiatry. What this really illustrates, as I've been emphasising, are the complex behaviours in organisations that can be the underlying source of problems. Without understanding them, and acting on them, they can sometimes prove fatal. Similar situations and major problems occur frequently in partnerships. They can have interesting dynamics, very similar to those in families, as they are a special family. But that is a story for another time.

Even though I have just scratched the surface our journey has come to an end, and, as I said in the introduction. I hope you found it different to conventional texts on management. That you found it interesting and, hopefully, at least in parts thought provoking and rewarding. Once again, sorry for all the I's.

More importantly, I hope that it has given you some ideas and means by which you can better understand organisations and make sense of what could be happening to you, and around you, in the organisations that you encounter in your life.

To take you further in your organisational life, you can check the following appendix.

Hitchhikers Guide to Intergalactic Organisational Analysis & Development

Earth Edition Workbook and Toolbox

Serious Stuff to think about and think about doing!

It pokes fun at lots of aspects of organisational life but has a lot of good stuff to do. It is by its nature prescriptive, but not too prescriptive!

FIN

Hitchhikers Guide to Intergalactic Organisational Analysis & Development

Earth Edition Workbook and Toolbox

A satirical light-hearted look at Organisations & Serious Stuff to think about and maybe think about doing!

DAVID PARIS

Structures and Dysfunctional Structural Shenanigans

The Byzantine Matrix

A bewildering structure with multiple reporting lines leaving employees unsure who their actual boss is and creating endless opportunities for accountability to fall through the cracks.

Departmental Turf Wars

Departments operate as little fiefdoms, prioritizing their goals over the good of the entire organisation. Competition trumps collaboration.

Silos of Isolation

Strict hierarchies and departmental divisions discourage cross functional communications leading to hoarding and redundant efforts.

Title Inflation Epidemic

An obsession with fancy titles ("Vice President of Strategic Initiatives" for someone managing three people), that mask a lack of influence or real decision-making power.

The Phantom Layer

Layers of middle management that seemingly exist for the sole purpose of relaying messages up and down, with difficult to decipher and detrimental delays and distortions.

Change for Change's Sake

Reorganizations become more frequent than strategy updates. A knee-jerk reaction to problems rather than a solution. Employees exhibit whiplash and cynicism.

The Invisible Org Chart

The official org chart looks neat and logical on paper, while the real power dynamics and lines of informal influence remain a closely guarded secret.

Job Description? What's that?

Job roles are so convoluted, or constantly changing that employees spend half their time figuring out what they are really responsible for and who else might be doing the same tasks.

Growth Gone Wild

Rapid expansion without adjusting the structure. Its like a gangly teenager suddenly sporting extra limbs, awkward, uncoordinated, clumsy and prone to accidents.

Ghost Departments

Some departments from a long-forgotten era linger on the org chart but no one knows *quite* what they do anymore, or even if they still exist.

Some Consequences and Fallout

Hiring Havoc

Unclear reporting lines and overlapping roles make it challenging to determine where new talent is needed, leading to mismatched hires or critical positions remaining unfilled.

The Accountability Void

Problems and questions ping-pong between departments, morphing into a blame game instead of getting solved.

Death of or Dubious Decision Making

With role confusion, buck passing and backside protection, decisions can be delayed and redirected until they disappear into the accountability and responsibility void.

More Seriously-A Structural Template

Start with Strategy

Articulate your organisation overarching mission, vision, and strategic goals.

What specific skills and workflows are vital to achieve these goals?

Work Breakdown Structure

- Detail the activities needed to deliver products or achieve your goals.
- Break this down into department's, functions, or teams based on specialisation.

Designate Roles and Responsibilities

- Craft clear job descriptions, for each position within your structure.
- Define authority and reporting lines (who reports to whom).

Consider these core structures:-

Functional: Organise employees by specialty e.g. sales, marketing, finance.

Divisional: Based on products/services, markets, or geographic regions.

Matrix: Blends functional and divisional- employees may report to two managers.

Flat: Fewer hierarchical layers, encouraging autonomy and quick decision-making.

Map communication channels

- Formal, regular reporting, team meetings, company intranet and informal.

Plan for agility and change

Review your structure as your business grows and goals evolve.

- Build in mechanisms to handle changes and shifts without major disruption.

Choosing the right structure.

Here are some basic factors impacting your choice:-

Size and Complexity: Larger organisations generally need more specialised roles and layers.

Strategy: An innovation driven firm might thrive in a flatter structure, while a highly regulated industry might lean towards a more controlled hierarchical one.

Culture: Your desired work culture may be better supported by a particular structure.

Tips

Involve Your Employees: get insights from various levels to understand the workflow and interdependencies.

Use Visual Tools: Org chart software makes it easy to visualise the structure and spot potential bottlenecks.

Start Simple: It's easier to layer on complexity as needed than deal with unnecessary bureaucracy.

Communicate Clearly: Rolling out a new structure requires communication and transparency to ensure adoption.

Common Pitfalls to Avoid

Rigid Silos: Avoid structures that inhibit cross functional collaboration.

Ambiguous Authority: Confusion about who makes decisions can stifle progress.

Underestimating people: Give employees the necessary authority to excel within their roles.

Neglecting Culture: Your structure should naturally support the type of environment and culture you wish to foster.

Creating the "Best" culture on the planet!

Creating the "Best" culture is tricky – what's incredible for one team might be a disaster for another but let's look at a few fundamentals!

Ditch the common Corporate Approach! Organisations are multicultural.

Don't be afraid to be different!

Beware of Generic Values and Mission Statements. Instead build a culture grounded in what makes your team special, be it sales, finance, IT or product development!

Define Core Values. Involve your employees in defining 3-5 values that will shape your culture's DNA e.g. integrity, innovation, collaboration, people focus, customer focus.

Understand that "best" is subjective. There is no universal template for an amazing culture. It's what feels right for your team, mission, and industry.

Culture Contract. Culture must be lived and not just plastered on office walls.

Psychological Safety. Create an environment where people feel secure enough to voice even radical ideas, offer constructive criticism and take healthy risks.

Build Genuine Trust. From leadership down to the frontline, fostering teamwork, initiative and achievement.

Shared Purpose Matters. A real sense of meaning and believing in the work goes way beyond wages and salaries.

Humour. Finding ways to infuse work with laughter can lower stress, soften tough moments and build camaraderie.

Appreciation. Recognition isn't just about bonuses. Its celebrating those everyday wins that make a difference, and valuing contributions of each person's role.

Fun that Isn't Forced. Finding activities that genuinely resonate with your team and are not just ticking a culture box.

Hire for Human and Train for Skill. Seek people that align with your culture first, specific skills can often be learned later.

Don't Hire Brilliant Misfits. One disruptive personality can poison an entire team. Prioritise character and collaboration skills rather than merely technical superstar status.

Beyond the Mentor. Encourage knowledge sharing and informal development across experience levels with access to staff who exemplify your culture.

Embrace Difference. It's team members with unconventional approaches that spark fresh thinking.

Encourage Time Out. Recognise the real risk of burnout, and the potential for related mental health, providing awareness sessions and risk-free access to help.

Lead From the Heart and Not the Bureaucracy. Inspire through actions and exemplify the company values.

Forge Feedback Loops for Course Correction. Keep channels open for receiving feedback as the company grows and changes.

Show Humility in the Face of Mistakes. Leaders are not perfect they can fail like others. Acknowledging it fosters trust and accountability.

Culture is Fluid. It requires constant attention and adaptability, not a one-time program so often seen.

Walk the Walk. If leaders don't model the required behaviours nobody else will.

Involve your Team. Co-creating aspects and features of your culture ensures a deeper buy-in and commitment.

Cultural Exchange Programs. Connect with other organisations with distinct or great cultures for inspiration and shared learning.

Organisational Observations and Culture Curiosities

The Mission Statement: A Work of Fantasy? Every company has one. It usually involves words like innovation, excellence, and customer centric. Pay no attention to the fact that the last time your company had a truly innovative idea was when someone suggested putting cup holders on the swivel chairs. The mission statement often only exists in a parallel universe where work is always thrilling, and every employee feels like Steve Jobs on his best day.

Corporate Buzzwords: Because Plain English is Too Easy. Let's circle back, think outside the box, leverage our synergies - such phrases are the verbal equivalent of numbing music played while you wait on a phone call. They are designed to make it sound like important things are happening, even if everyone is slightly unsure what those things are.

Performance Reviews: The Dance of The Delicate Ego. The annual ritual where managers must delicately inform employees that they are both indispensable, and in need of improvement. Phrases like areas for opportunity, and room for growth, mask the real questions. How big of a raise will I not be getting, and can I start looking for a new job discreetly during my extra-long lunch break?

Office Politics: Subtler Than Game of Thrones. Who sits closest to the window? Who gets invited to the important sounding, yet mysterious meetings? Office politics are alive and well, fuelled by strategic lunch buddies and an unspoken code decipherable only by those with at least five years at the company.

Flexibility Mirage: Proclaiming work-life balance and flexible work arrangements, all while subtly penalising anyone who uses them.

Forced Fun: Mandatory "team building" activities that are awkward, uninspired and make everyone wish they were back at their desks.

The Sacred Tradition: Mindlessly carrying on outdated company rituals such as employee of the month, even when it's no longer wanted or relevant.

The Unspoken Dress Code: Despite there being no official dress code, it becomes clear there are subtle unwritten rules about what is "acceptable" leading to unnecessary conformity.

"We're a Family" Trap: Using the family metaphor to promote team togetherness but blurring professional boundaries and fostering an expectation of overwork or self-sacrifice.

The Great Pretend: Publicly touting "core values" that sound lovely on the web site but bear little resemblance to how the organisation really operates.

The Email Avalanche: Every minor point requires an email, with escalating cc: chains until half the company is debating the lunch menu in your inbox.

The Jargon Jungle: Leaders who communicate exclusively in buzzwords and management-speak, leaving everyone scrambling for an online business acronym decoder.

The Reply-All Apocalypse: That one coworker who loves hitting "Reply All" for utterly irrelevant messages, ensuring a productivity-sucking email vortex.

The Information Black Hole: Critical announcements made in impromptu hallway conversations, ensuring that those out of the office or working remotely are left totally clueless.

Toxic Cultures and Fallout

Enron: A poster child for corporate fraud, greed, and a culture of deception. Employees were encouraged to cut corners, hide losses, and manipulate accounting to achieve short-term goals. This led to one of the biggest financial scandals in history and long imprisonment of the CEO.

Wells Fargo Bank: The pressure to meet unrealistic sales goals led employees to create millions of fake accounts for customers. This culture of cross-selling at any cost damaged the banks reputation and led to massive fines.

Uber under Kalanick: During Kalanick's leadership Uber cultivated a "bro culture" with rampant sexism, harassment, and a disregard for ethics and regulations. This toxic culture harmed employees and contributed to public scandals.

Volkswagen: The company's obsession with becoming the worlds largest automaker fostered a culture where cheating on emissions tests was acceptable. This blatant disregard for environmental standards deeply damaged Volkswagen's reputation and resulted in billions of dollars in fines.

USA Gymnastics: The Larry Nassar sexual abuse scandal exposed a toxic culture where athlete safety was ignored, and reports of abuse silenced. Leaders prioritised medals and reputation, over the well-being of the gymnasts they were supposed to protect.

The Catholic Church: Decades of systematic cover-ups and a culture of protecting abusers, and the institution, led to a global crisis of faith, but far worse to the death of possibly hundreds of victims. In addition, thousands of victims and their families were permanently damaged. This is ongoing and continues to affect the institution and those of the faith.

These examples received international publicity, but such behaviours have all been widely experienced and publicly denounced in Australian corporations and institutions. Indeed, they have been, and are still being seen worldwide.

Toxic Culture Common Threads

Unethical Leadership: Leaders set the tone. When those in power prioritise profits or self-interest over ethics and integrity, this can, or does become, a guiding principle for the whole organisation.

Win-at-All-Costs Mentality: Extreme pressure to hit targets, regardless of how they are achieved, breeds unethical and dishonest behaviour and ethical rules don't apply. This emboldens and encourage further misconduct.

Fear and Silence: Employees are afraid to speak up about problems due to retaliation. This may be from peers, loss of employment, or worse. We have seen internationally, with Julian Assange being an example, and with David McBride in Australia, of the serious risks, both financial and imprisonment, that can be faced by whistleblowers.

Important Note: Organisations are made up of people and mistakes happen. What separates a bad decision from a toxic culture is the ongoing pattern of behaviour, the leadership's response and the impact on the people involved.

So, you want to become a fantastic leader?

Questions on leading and leadership have been asked and discussed for thousands of years. At the heart of most questions was the fundamental one asking whether leaders were born or made. The outcome of the vast amount or research on this topic, is that leaders are generally made, based on the social environment that surrounds them, and moulded from situations they have been in, where certain skills or knowledge have come to the fore. This has certainly been my experience. I was very happy in my youth, and early business career, to be a follower and shied away from the responsibility of leader roles. I've never wanted to be a leader or achieve power. However, in quite a few situations in the military, in business and in my academic career I fell into the role of leader. In every case the leader role was given to me. Importantly, in every case I was comfortable in the leader role and felt confident I had the ability required to lead. Thus, in those situations leading came naturally, and I filled the roles effectively. Why was this? In my view it was simply in those situations or circumstances, the knowledge, skills and confidence in my ability was recognised by my peers This made it natural and easy for me to assume the leader role, with their unspoken consent.

Becoming a great leader is a journey of personal development and dedication to continuous learning. I can give you a basic guide combining essential qualities with some practical actions you can take!

First let's Take a Humorous look at Leaders and Leadership

The Visionary: Has grand ideas with zero understanding of how anything gets done. Catch phrases include, disruptive paradigm shifts, and let's blue-sky this!

The Ghost: Rarely seen, mostly heard of in hushed tones. Pronouncements come down on high, usually via confusing company-wide emails at 4:55 PM on a Friday.

The Cheerleader: Endlessly optimistic, to the point of delusion. Insists everything is fantastic, even when the office printer is on fire and half the team has resigned.

The "I Used to do Your Job": Can't resist the urge to take over, showing you exactly how to format that Excel spreadsheet like they did back in '07.

Drinking the Red Bull: Used to describe unquestioning, cult-like adherence to the company line, even if the company line makes no sense.

Right Sizing: The corporate euphemism for firing people.

Let's Take This Off-Line: Translation: I'm about to say something controversial/ critical/I don't want documented in an email chain.

Looking at Your Core Attributes

Self-Awareness: Honest self-awareness of your strengths, weaknesses. Leaders aren't perfect but they recognise where they excel and where they need support. Know how you are perceived by others. Try asking!

Understanding your Tendencies: We all have blind spots and irritating habits. Actively seek feedback and know how your actions impact your team or members.

Recognise your Language Needs: Master the art of clear, purposeful communications in a language that connects with different styles and personalities as well as their goals and challenges.

Integrity: Be honest, ethical, trustworthy, and follow through on promises. Model the behaviour you expect from others. Your moral compass sets the tone for the entire team.

Be a True Visionary: Have a clear sense of where you want to go, what you want to achieve, and the direction you want to take. Articulate the big vision and get people excited about it. Be able to communicate your vision clearly and inspire others to want to work with you to reach a shared goal.

Empathy: Understand the emotions and needs of your team. Build genuine connections and personalise your leadership style being sensitive to individuals who often have different needs. Demonstrate genuine care for your team as their well-being is crucial to your mission success. How much do you really know about them?

Decisiveness: Be confident in your ability to make decisions, even under pressure. Don't let the fear of making mistakes paralyse you, and don't be afraid to seek wisdom and guidance from others.

Growth Orientation: Embrace learning, readily adapt to change and foster a learning environment for your team. Allow them to make mistakes while learning. Risk taking and resilience are forged through experience.

Be like a Chameleon: Adapt quickly to changing environments whether internal or external and find unexpected opportunities in new circumstances.

Action Steps you can take!

Find Mentors: Identify leaders you admire or respect. If possible, seek their guidance and learn from their successes and failures. If not, you have biographies or autobiographies you can research.

Develop your skills: Improve your communication, decision making, problem solving, conflict resolution, strategic thinking capabilities and other skills through training workshops or on-line programs.

Listen Actively: Really listen to, really hear, and address your team's concerns, ideas, and feedback. Make them feel heard and valued.

Empower your team: Delegate responsibility along with any necessary authority and trust them to do their jobs by guiding them without micro-managing.

Recognise achievement: Celebrate individual and team wins. Acknowledge effort and show real appreciation.

Be Accountable: Own your mistakes and take responsibility for your actions. This builds trust and respect. Disowning and buck-passing do the opposite.

Promote a positive culture: Continually foster a sense of collaboration, respect, trust and inclusivity where your team members feel safe and are encouraged to take risks and grow.

Grow your Replacements: Identify team members who flourish with autonomy and entrust them with meaningful responsibility. Use feedback loops as tools not weapons to review progress, give guidance and empower autonomy.

Additional Actions

Reflect regularly: Set aside time to reflect on your leader style, the challenges you face, and areas for further development. Inviting and receiving honest feedback is invaluable in this process.

Read Widely: Explore books and articles on leading and leadership, along with the associated philosophies and cultures espoused or fostered. Cases studies illustrating successes and failures can be invaluable.

Network: Connect with leaders you respect, admire or would like to emulate within and outside your organisation to exchange ideas and activities.

Remember

Becoming a great leader isn't about being perfect. Its about a continuous commitment to vision, growth, learning, achievement, adaptability and most important; putting your people first. Humility is also nice. Sadly, not my forte but I also mock myself ruthlessly to compensate!

And Some Strategies if All Else Fails!

Blame someone else and hope no one notices.

Try randomly promoting people until something good happens.

Write a strongly worded memo all in uppercase. That always demonstrates strong leadership skills!

Change the company's slogan to something vague and aspirational. No one will notice things are falling apart.

Reschedule everything as "strategic planning sessions" and order lots of pizza.

Start using more buzzwords. If they sound indecipherable enough people will assume you're brilliant.

Stare out the window meaningfully and pretend you're contemplating a really complex problem.

Try delegating your job to the office plant. Can't be any worse than what you're doing, right?

Abysmal Leadership Hall of Fame

The Seagull Manager: They swoop in sporadically, make a lot of noise, squark orders, leave a mess, and vanish until the next crisis.

The Credit Thief: They eagerly take credit for any team successes while deftly assigning blame for failures to unfortunate subordinates.

The "My Way or Highway" Dictator: Rigidly attached to their own ideas, viewing disagreements or suggestions as personal attacks. They create a culture of fear, not collaboration and innovation. We have looked at some of these.

The Master of Inconsistencies: Their directives change with the wind, leaving employees confused and demoralised. Yesterday's priority is today's irrelevant task.

The Communication Ghost: Important information never trickles down. Employees are expected to magically divine expectations or be blamed for not knowing.

The Teflon Leader: Never accountable for their own mistakes or bad decisions; excuses flow effortlessly while team members shoulder the consequences.

The Lip Service Initiatives: Holding innovation or autonomy workshops that just pay lip service to the idea with no concrete action plans.

The Bias Free Bias: Claiming to be bias free while constantly exhibiting bias in hiring, promotions, workplace relations and interactions.

Leadership Lowlights

"Open Door" Policy that Isn't: Leaders who proclaim to have an open-door policy while subtly, or not so subtly, discouraging anyone from using it.

Performance Review Charades: Annual reviews filled with vague, recycled feedback that offers no actual insight or guidance.

The Inspirational Quote Enthusiast: The leader who believes plastering generic motivational quotes on the walls is a substitute genuine leadership and clear direction.

Vision Statement Enigma: Lofty company mission statements, riddled with corporate jargon, yet strangely unclear about what the company really does.

Micromanager on Parade: The leader obsessed with minutiae and unable to trust employees to do their jobs without constant interventions or handholding.

The best example of this that I encountered was when asked by the CEO of a major corporation if I could coach a senior manager in writing "correct" business letters. The manager concerned was fantastic in his job, but the pedantic CEO was reading all the letters he wrote and correcting them for syntax and punctuation before being posted. I met the manager, a great guy and fully aware of his writing deficiencies. The coaching sessions were very short lived. I simply told the manager to stop writing letters and use fax, text or terse emails to bypass the CEO. My shortest ever consulting job! It worked!

Goals and Goal Displacement

A primary task for leaders and managers is to set the goals of the organisation. The goals are those required to be met to realise the organisation's purpose and mission. Subsidiary objectives and milestones are set to achieve the goals. Unfortunately, in many instances and in many organisations, we see goal displacement occur. Goal displacement is a sociological phenomenon, where the original goals of the organisation gradually get replaced by secondary goals. These often serve the self-interest of the organisation's members rather than the organisation and occur over time in the following ways.

Bureaucratisation: Over time, procedures, rules, and hierarchies emerge to maintain order and structure within the organisation.

Focus on Means over Ends: A growing emphasis on following these procedures and meeting bureaucratic requirements can cause employees to focus on the means rather than on the original purpose, mission and goals. This typically progresses to a focus on self-preservation and self-interest of members. The initial, broader social or economic goals of the organisation become subordinate to those of individuals.

New Goal Formation: The evolution of these individual focused self-preservation or career goals can, and frequently does, lead to a failure to achieve the original purpose and mission. Or, the achievement of the original goals requires far higher expenditure and costs being incurred, because of operational inefficiencies.

Goal displacement is far more frequent in government, quasi-government enterprises, as well as tertiary colleges, universities, not-for-profit and similar organisations. This is because in many cases performance targets and measures are vague, amorphous and mutable with responsibility for failure hard to assign.

Addressing and mitigating goal displacement is comparatively simple where true and fair metrics for performance and goal achievement can be established and measured. In most cases we are looking at quantitative measures across a whole range of possible activities. However, we still must be very careful on the measurements we adopt as there can easily be unintended consequences. These can include goal displacement because of the measures we adopt. For example.

In American universities it is not uncommon to use the statistical standard distribution to allocate pass, credit and distinction grades. Using the so-called Bell Curve is very controversial. However, forgetting the mathematical or statistical critiques, there emerged a very disturbing behavioural outcome in students. Under this statistical system you could increase your grade by other students getting lower grades. Firstly, this encouraged a culture of conflict rather than cooperation among students. It also led some students to steal, disfigure or remove all relevant or useful texts and journals from libraries and other sources. This meant they did, but their student competitors did not, have access to the resources. Where you have assessment programmes that measure the performance of students and schools you also get issues. The schools and the teachers focus principally on coaching students to pass the tests set by the testing authority. The broader normal and important educational curriculum and important behavioural, but unmeasured activities, become subordinate to the relatively narrow test. When "Management By Objectives", MBO, became the key performance measure in organisations it suffered similar and major problems. It focused on measurable goals and targets and put great stress on organisational members to meet them in a specific time frame It also frequently led to goal overload. However, it ignored other key features of a company. These included its culture, the conduct of employees, the healthy work ethos, the areas of involvement and contributions such as mentoring and other cooperative behaviours. It was the brain-child of Peter Drucker in the 1950's. It is questionable how relevant it is in its original form, but a need for measurement remains. More commonly now we see KPO's and KPI's. Key performance objectives and key performance indicators which are measures of performance that offer greater latitude.

Strategies to Combat Goal Displacement

Crystal Clear Goals and Values

Start with goals that are SMART, (Specific, Measurable, Achievable, Relevant, and Time-Bound)

Make sure the goals align deeply with the organisations core values and mission. A strong "why" is your north star guide.

Conduct Regular Check-ins and Course Correction

Build in regular reviews of progress towards goals. Are the actions being taken truly moving you closer to the desired outcome?

Don't be afraid to pivot. Rigidity in pursuit of outdated goals is just as harmful as goal displacement.

Metrics That Matter

Choose metrics that measure actual outcomes, not just activity. Don't get trapped in vanity metrics that look good but don't truly reflect impact.

Combine quantitative data with qualitative feedback and observations to get the full picture.

Emphasise Learning and Improvement

Celebrate not just reaching goals, but the process of getting there. What lessons were learned?

Create a culture where it's OK to experiment and where failure is seen as an opportunity to analyse and adjust, not a reason for blame.

Empowerment and Transparency

Involve team members at all levels in goal setting and decision making. This promotes ownership and keeps everyone connected to the bigger picture.

Open communication about both successes and challenges keeps everyone accountable and minimises the potential for misunderstandings.

Key Takeaway

Preventing goal displacement requires ongoing vigilance and the culture focused on the true purpose behind the work, rather than just blindly adhering to processes or metrics.

What About Rewards for Performance

As with every other aspect of managing organisations, we must be aware of the unintended consequences of every decision that we make. Using systems thinking will help avoid them. We can think about effective reward systems by looking at the unintended consequences of poorly designed ones.

The One-Size-Fits-None Prize: Rewards that fail to consider individual preferences. Everyone gets the same generic gift card or company branded swag, regardless of whether they find it valuable or motivating.

Emphasis on Competition: Reward systems that pit employees against each other, fostering a cutthroat environment instead of collaboration. Think sales leader boards with no recognition for teamwork.

Quantity over Quality: Rewarding the sheer volume of production, sales, work or hours clocked instead of performance quality. This encourages employees to cut corners, burnout, and see only the short term.

The Participation Award: Everybody gets a reward just for showing up. There's no distinction between average contributions and truly excellent work, demoralising high performers.

The Elusive Criteria: Goals or metrics for rewards are unclear or inconsistently applied. Employees end up confused and cynical about the entire process.

Key Features of Well-Designed Rewards

Meaningful and Desirable: The rewards must be things people want and value. This requires understanding your workforces needs and preferences.

Aligned with Goals: Rewards directly tied to specific performance goals, behaviours, or outcomes they intend to reinforce. Misalignment leads to mixed messages and confusion.

Equitable and Transparent: Fairness is crucial. Employees need clear performance expectations and a sense that rewards are distributed consistently based on merit.

Timely: The closer the reward follows the valued behaviour, the stronger the reinforcement it provides. Avoid delays that dilute the connection.

Varied and Flexible: A mix of reward types (financial, recreational, recognition, developmental) caters to diverse preferences. Offering choice within the system can be highly motivating.

Personalised: If possible, tailoring rewards to the individual increases their perceived value (e.g. some employees may refer a development opportunity over cash bonus).

Reward Examples

Financial: Bonuses, profit sharing, stock options, pay increases.

Recognition: Public praise, awards, nominations, visibility in company communications.

Experiential: Tickets to events, travel opportunities, changing roles or geographic locations.

Development: Monitoring, training, conference attendance, stretch assignments.

Flexibility: Extra time off, work from home options, choice of projects.

Important Design Considerations

Company Culture: Your reward system should fit your organisation's overall culture and values. A flashy, competitive system might work well in one company, but fall flat in another.

Budget: Be realistic about what your organisation can afford, both in terms of monetary rewards and non-financial offerings like time and development opportunities.

Communication and Celebration: A well designed reward system won't be effective if people don't know it exists! Communicate clearly about the available rewards, criteria for earning them, and celebrate success publicly.

Evolution: Regularly evaluate your reward systems effectiveness. What's working and what's not? Be open to adjustment based on feedback and changing needs.

Remember

Rewards are most powerful when they are seen as a sincere tool to recognise and reinforce behaviours that align with the organisation's goals' not just a transactional exchange.

Boundaries and Boundary Management

As a leader, a manager or simply as an individual with family and friends you are constantly managing boundaries. Boundary management is fundamental to systems thinking, and to all human interaction. It is a forever and vital skill, so we need to revisit it.

Understanding Types of Organisational Boundaries

Vertical Boundaries: Those that separate hierarchical levels such as shop floor staff, frontline supervisors and senior management. These focus on authority reporting lines and decision-making processes. All staff are involved in managing these boundaries.

Horizontal Boundaries: These divide the organisation into departments or functions (marketing, sales, finance etc). They emphasise specialisation and coordination between these areas. All staff are again importantly involved in managing these boundaries.

External Boundaries: Boundaries separating the organisation from external stakeholders like suppliers, customers, regulators, and competitors. They deal with information flow, perceptions, relationships, and the degree of collaboration or separation. Company members from senior managers, to purchasing officers, to sales staff, the receptionist at the front desk, or the staff members serving customers. All are managing important external boundaries.

Geographic Boundaries: These are relevant if your organisation has multiple locations or operates internationally. They can involve managing differences in language, customs, cultures, regulations, ethics, laws and time zones among others.

Why Managing Boundaries Well Matters

Relationships: We all know that our relationships with others, whether they be individuals or companies, are an outcome of how well we manage our boundaries. At the end of the day nearly all boundary management comes down to managing interactions between people.

Efficiency: Well defined boundaries can prevent duplication of effort, streamline processes, and improve our resource allocation.

Clear Accountability: Clear boundaries establish responsibilities for different activities and the goals associated with those activities. They also foster good working relationships with other departments.

Conflict Resolution: Ambiguous boundaries often lead to misunderstandings, disowned responsibilities, turf wars, frustration and other dysfunctional outcomes.

Organisational Success: Well managed boundaries are key to successful relationships within the organisation and externally with clients, suppliers and regulators.

Let's Revisit Groups and Teams

Teams can be seen as distinct from groups in the way the public views them principally in the sporting arena. However, they are just groups but deemed to have special characteristics.

Positives for Groups and Teams

Collective Goal Orientation: A strong sense of shared purpose motivates and aligns members.

Synergy: Combining diverse skills and perspectives can unlock solutions that surpass what individuals can achieve alone. It's a case of members performing at the best of their ability and where the collective potential can greatly exceed the sum of the individual members.

Diverse Skills and Perspectives Include: Varied backgrounds, skill sets, and knowledge, offering rich brainstorming opportunities and better overall problem- solving abilities.

Increased Creativity and Innovation: Collaboration sparks ideas that single individuals wouldn't generate alone. Diverse viewpoints prevent stale, unimaginative thinking, and challenge questionable assumptions.

Mutual Accountability: Members hold each other responsible for their performance, fostering a commitment to quality.

Boosted Morale and Belonging: Teamwork provides camaraderie, a sense of shared purpose, and fosters a feeling of belonging within larger organisations. This improves job satisfaction and member retention.

Shared Workload and Support: Tasks get distributed amongst members, making large projects manageable. Team members can provide support, mentoring, and pick up the slack in challenging situations.

Support and Growth: Teams provide a space for mutual learning, mentorship, and building strong professional relationships.

Possible Negatives for Groups and Teams

Conflict Potential: Diverse opinions and personalities can clash. Differences in work styles, or lack of clear roles can lead to friction that slows down decision making and undermines effective collaboration. Effective conflict resolution skills are essential.

Dominant Individuals: A few outspoken members may influence the group disproportionately, silencing valuable input, and possibly resulting in adverse outcomes.

Social Loafing: Some individuals may contribute less effort when part of a larger group, assuming others will pick up their share. This can frustrate high performing team members. Removal of social loafers is a good idea.

Diffusion of Responsibility: When decision making and its consequences are spread across individuals in a team, taking personal responsibility, ownership, and accountability can be diminished. This is how some individuals remove their responsibility for taking decisions that they should be taking.

Groupthink: In the quest for cohesion, teams may suppress critical thinking and dissenting opinions. This hampers or blocks a wider exploration of possible options or solutions, and leads to poor decision making, and potentially dangerous outcomes. Groupthink is a social and psychological phenomenon. It is where the desire for harmony and conformity within a group, overrides critical thinking and rational decision making. Individual members suppress their doubts, disagreements, and alternative viewpoints, to maintain a perceived unanimous agreement and avoid conflict. It was first explored and developed as a theory by social psychologist Irving Janis in his book "Victims of Groupthink: A Psychological Study of Foreign Policy Decisions and Fiascoes". I really recommend this to you. It discusses thinking, policy and action decisions involved in such major events as the invasion of Pearl Harbour, the Bay of Pigs invasion of Cuba, and the Cuban Missile Crisis between the United States and Russia, that could have led to World War 3. Later examples are considered to include the Challenger Space Shuttle Disaster and The Iraq War.

Groupthink characteristics are commonly encountered in organisations so we need to look at Groupthink in more detail.

Groupthink and its Key Characteristics

Illusion of Invulnerability: An excessive sense of optimism and overestimation of the group's capabilities, leading to unwarranted risk taking.

Collective Rationalisation: Justifying or downplaying warning signs and minimising the possible negative consequences of decisions.

Belief in Moral Superiority: Believing the group's decisions are inherently ethical and righteous regardless of any counter evidence.

Stereotyping Out-Groups: Dismissive and prejudicial views of potential opponents or rivals diminishing their ability to pose a genuine threat.

Pressure on Dissenters: Members self-censor and those expressing minority opinions are met with subtle or overt disapproval, ensuring continued conformity.

Illusion of Unanimity: Silence is falsely interpreted as agreement, and the lack of opposition reinforces the false notion of consensus.

Serious Consequences of Groupthink

Poor Decision-Making: Flawed choices arise from a lack of thorough evaluation of risks, disregard for alternative solutions, and failure to examine possible negative outcomes.

Ethical Lapses: The group's self-perception of morality can blind them to unethical consequences of their actions.

Stifled Creativity: Groupthink suppresses original ideas, dissent, and innovative thinking, limiting potential solutions.

Preventing Groupthink

Establishing the Group Culture: It is the culture and norms of the group that will dictate how effectively it works. The leader needs to establish and demonstrate these. In Janis's book he tells how President John Kennedy realised he had to absent himself from many of the group discussions. He did this as he was concerned that too many group members were saying what they thought he wanted to hear. Not what they believed. Removing himself resolved that problem.

Encouraging Diverse Viewpoints: Actively seek out perspectives from outside the group and encourage membership from varied backgrounds to join the team.

Devil's Advocate Role: This is important. Assign a member to challenge prevailing assumptions and offer alternative viewpoints to stimulate critical thinking. Someone having this specific role is vital. Without this role, dissent, questioning assumptions, opinions or beliefs can be self-censored or undeclared due to group norms and the fear of reprisal.

Open Discussion and Dissent: Leaders must clearly prioritise open and honest discussion, ensuring dissenting voices are heard and valued.

Subgroups: Breakdown large groups into smaller teams for brainstorming to prevent premature consensus and enable more candid ideas.

Anonymous Feedback: There may still be members who are insecure, afraid to question others and fearful of ridicule. So, provide options for confidential feedback or critiques to ensure their concerns can be expressed and then openly discussed.

Groups Norms and Breaking Them

Think about groups of which you have been or currently are a member. Think about the number of times you have observed the behaviours described, and the times that your behaviour in them has been described. Also think about how you might change things.

Throughout my career I've been a norm breaker in general and in groups. It can be very challenging, risky and is incredibly difficult. Think of the number of times you have wanted to say something or behave in a particular way but have not done so. Mostly this is due to the behavioural norms that we have internalised. Alcohol and drugs of course can remove the inhibitions those norms impose on our behaviour.

I'll just recount two examples. I'd flown 4000 kilometres to attend an international accounting congress. It comprised principal speakers at plenary sessions and sub-groups addressing accounting specialties or research topics. There were about 400 accountants attending the plenary sessions. In one session the presenter was giving a paper on cost accounting. I listened intently trying to understand what he was talking about, but it made no sense whatsoever. At one point, part way through, the moderator, a famous professor of accounting who had written several widely used textbooks, asked whether there were any questions. I stood up, one out of four hundred, feeling extremely tense and exposed, and said "I have no idea what this presenter is talking about. It is making no sense at all, and I'd like to know why we are listening"? There was a hushed silence, followed by a loud outbreak of voices from the participants, and the moderator was running up the stairs to confront me! He arrived and to my total surprise, as I was shaking like a leaf, he shook my hand and congratulated me, saying "thank God you had the courage to intervene. I had no idea what he was talking about either. It was gobbledegook". Later, over drinks at the hotel, many other participants congratulated me. The really interesting thing is that once a norm has been broken it is far easier for others to break it. Participants after this incident raised many questions with subsequent speakers. This is why authoritarian regimes come down so hard on anyone who in any way questions or breaches the party imperatives.

The second time was at meeting of some 150 university academic staff organised by the union. A resolution was proposed to take an action with a vote by raising hands of those for and those opposed. I was the only one opposed and could feel the group pressure from everyone to take down my hand and make it unopposed. I couldn't and got many angry looks.

Careers and Getting Ahead- This is about You!

Grovel Your Way to the Top

Many years ago, I was watching an episode of the English BBC comedy "The Good Life" when the layback good lifer, Tom Good, asked his corporate neighbour, Jerry Leadbetter, how he had advanced his career to be a senior executive. His response was "I grovelled my way to the top"! I loved that comment. It stayed with me and disappointingly I've seen that strategy work too often in the real world. It has always, in my experience, been in public institutions and bureaucracies, where goals, standards, and measures of personal achievement are amorphous and ephemeral. Universities are classic examples of where I've seen the strategy work quite often.

Alternative Paths to Leadership

Leadership: Even early on, lead projects, step up and offer solutions beyond your role. True leaders act on initiatives before promotion forces them to.

Emotional Intelligence: Master self-awareness, cultivate empathy, and skilfully navigate office politics and conflict resolution for increased influence.

Become an Exceptional Contributor: Go above and beyond. Deliver consistently excellent work and become known for reliability.

Expertise: Become the go-to in your field. Pursue continuous learning, embrace mentorship, and build a reputation as a master of your craft.

Focus on Relationship Building: Develop meaningful professional connections by mentoring, helping others, and being authentic. People support those they have strong bonds with.

Strategic Thinking: Elevate yourself beyond tasks to see the big picture. Get the helicopter view. Understand how your role connects to company goals and how decisions impact the whole organisation.

Strategic Networking: Attend industry events, connect with thought leaders online, and actively seek out valuable contacts while genuinely offering something in return.

Core Leadership Principles

Authenticity Matters: People spot fake interest from far away. Build relationships based on genuine curiosity, helpfulness, and shared interests.

Give Before You Get: Networking is not just about what you can gain. Think about how you can offer value to others - provide insights, connect people, or share helpful resources.

Long Term Focus: Successful relationships take time to develop. Don't view networking as a transactional exchange; Instead, be patient and focus on building trust.

Quality over Quantity: Rather than collecting meaningless business cards, focus on forging deep connections with a select few people who can meaningfully impact your career path and vice versa.

Navigating The Organisation

Be Visible: Volunteer for high profile projects, present at meetings, and proactively share your achievements (without arrogance of course).

Find Sponsors: Identify supportive senior staff who are invested in your development and will advocate for you when opportunities arise.

Take Intelligent Risks: Step outside your comfort zone, seek stretch assignments, or initiate challenging projects that demonstrate your capabilities.

Embrace Feedback. Welcome feedback, both positive and negative, as a development tool. Respond to criticism with actionable steps for improvement.

Demonstrate Commitment: Show dedication to the organisation mission and willingness to make sacrifices when needed. Don't overlook the risk of burnout.

Problem Solver Mentality. Don't simply identify issues, develop solutions and present compelling pitches backed by data and insight.

Exceed Expectations: Consistently deliver exceptional work, under-promise, and over-deliver on assigned tasks and timelines.

Be Adaptable: Thrive in ever-evolving environments. Embrace change with willingness to pivot, and help others see opportunities hidden within shifting realities.

Champion Others: Mentorship, and helping others around you succeed, reinforces your leadership while strengthening relationships.

Some Hard Truths

Politics Are Real: Even companies preaching meritocracy are influenced by office politics. Know who holds informal power and focus on fostering respectful alliances.

Luck Plays a Role: Your timing matters. Even with perfect execution, a merger, shifting company direction, or staff changes, can temporarily block your path. Patience is a key.

It's Not Just About You: Building genuine camaraderie and a reputation for helping others succeed goes further than mere self-promotion.

Let's Be Honest

There is no universal path to the top of an organisation. Company culture, your industry, who you know, and a bit of good fortune all contribute to a career trajectory.

Relationship Building Tips

The Art of Follow Up: following up after meetings shows genuine interest. It could be sharing a relevant article, connecting them to your network, or even a simple personalised thank you note.

Listen actively: Give people your full attention during conversations. Ask thoughtful questions and make a point to remember details, building genuine rapport.

Maintain Touchpoints: Don't let connections go dormant. Periodic check-ins, celebrating their successes or offering help, even on small matters, strengthens the bond.

Career Pitfalls

The Burnout Sacrifice: Putting every waking hour into work with self-deprivation to show dedication. This risks physical/mental decline while creating unsustainable expectations you can't maintain long term. It can also damage personal relationships.

Values Blindspot: Chasing any advancement with no assessment of if the company or leadership aligns with your ethics.

You could reach the top of an organisation you ultimately find morally reprehensible. I experienced this in the so called ethical pharmaceutical industry that proved far from ethical. Purdue Pharma and the Oxycontin opioid epidemic in the United States is a case in point. Over 100,000 US citizens died from Oxycontin overdoses in 2022 alone.

Overspecialisation: Becoming so niche that if your specialisation falls out of favour or tech disrupts it, you are left with non-transferable skills, limiting internal options.

Yes-Machine Complex: Saying yes to everything to please supervisors, becoming overloaded, and ultimately delivering mediocre work that hurts more than if you'd set boundaries early on.

Waiting For Recognition: Assuming if you do an amazing job, it will be discovered organically. You often **need** to advocate for yourself to be considered for growth. Find ways to strategically highlight your wins or strengths.

Caution: There's a fine line between self-promotion and bragging. Focus on the impact of your work, not just on how awesome you are.

Release Your Inner Innovator

Mindset Matters

Embrace Curiosity: Become genuinely fascinated by things. Ask questions, dig deeper, and challenge the status quo. Why does it work this way? And what if? Are powerful starting points.

Redefine Failure: See setbacks as learning opportunities, not catastrophes. Each failure brings you closer to a potential solution. Thomas Edison famously quipped "I have not failed I've just found 10,000 ways that won't work".

Play is Essential: Embrace childlike wonder. Allow yourself to experiment, daydream, and tinker. Some of the most groundbreaking ideas came from just "messing around".

Practical Habits

Get Out of Your Bubble: consciously expose yourself to new ideas, industries, and ways of thinking. Attend conferences or workshops outside your normal domain, travel, or mingle with people from different backgrounds.

Become An Observer: Observe your surroundings with a critical eye. Look for inefficiencies, pain points, people experiences, or needs that aren't met, innovation is often driven by solving real-world problems. The first outboard motor was developed by Evinrude in 1907. On a picnic he had rowed a boat across a lake to get an ice-cream for his son. Despite rowing fast to get back, the ice-cream had melted and he was exhausted. He decided there had to be a better way, and there was!

Collaborate Across Boundaries: Innovation thrives on the intersection of different perspectives. Break out of department silos and actively seek insights from people with diverse expertise.

Rapid Prototyping: Don't get bogged down by perfectionism. Embrace a test and learn approach, by creating rough prototypes or simulations to quickly get feedback and refine your ideas. Remember Edison took well over a thousand prototypes to get a reliable incandescent bulb.

I'd love to be able to describe some of the innovative ideas and projects that I and my close friends financed in the heady days of a stock market boom. Suffice to say that they included a rotary internal combustion engine, toroidal propulsion systems with the potential for submarines to travel quietly at unheard of speeds, and the development of concepts first discussed by Nicola Tesla. I even brought a Tesla coil to Australia. We had some hilarious moments of failure. Our rotary combustion engine was repurposed as an air motor, and the manufacturing rights sold to Ingersoll Rand. With Tesla in mind, go and stand under cross country high voltage electrical power transmission lines with a fluorescent tube in your hand. It will light up!

Try to Innovate and Influence Organisational Support

Psychological Safety: Create an environment where experimentation and calculated risks are celebrated, not punished. People need to feel comfortable suggesting out of the box ideas.

Dedicated Time: Provide time and resources for employees to explore innovation, whether its small slices carved out of regular work or "hackathon" like events. 3M is a great example of a company that encourages employees to be creative with 15% of their time. Creative projects are called "skunkwork" 3M has over 60,000 products many created and designed by staff. A famous one is "Post Its". A trial of a new adhesive product had failed but some enterprising staff had an idea. They made pads of notepaper using the failed adhesive and sent them around 3M to be used for note taking. Soon they were in big demand from across the company and from this came the successful major product line of "Post Its". Great success was achieved by creative staff from a repurposed failed adhesive!

Cross Functional Teams: Encourage teams comprised of different skill sets and departmentally backgrounds to tackle complex problems with fresh perspectives.

Important Notes

Innovation is a journey: It's not a singular Eureka moment. Practice makes perfect when it comes to cultivating an innovative mindset.

Inspiration is Everywhere: Pay attention to successful innovations from other industries. Could a similar concept be adapted or improved for your field?

Making Good Decisions and Considering Risk

We do need to be good at making decisions, and for this we need to understand risk. In my experience, and that of many business owners I have talked with, risk is a key factor they evaluate, with all important decisions. And the perceived risk will be influenced by their risk profile. We all have a risk profile. It has a major role on decisions we are willing to take. A risk profile is not fixed. It can change over time with experiences and in different circumstances.

In a workshop at the London School of Economic this was a topic addressed with a group of about twenty-five successful businessmen. Without exception they agreed that they were far more risk averse than when they had started their companies. The reasons they all gave were that when they started, they had virtually nothing to lose, plus if the business failed, they had plenty of time to recover. As a result, they were ready to take big risks. Now things had changed. They had a lot to lose, and they no longer had the same time available to recover from any loss. As a result, they were far more risk averse. However, they were only risk averse if they were seriously risking their lifestyles or their businesses. In addition, of course, they had no need to take major risks as they had achieved their goals. The same situation can apply in our personal lives. A reason why the rich get richer, is that they can take many more and larger risks in new ventures or investments, as a loss would have a negligible impact on their lives. Risk taking is an essential part of life. Risk taking is not gambling or speculating. Risk taking is about making calculated decisions, after the probabilities and impact of positive and negative outcomes have been considered, and calculated if it is possible. It is not always possible, and some decisions and actions require a leap of faith. Another aspect of risk is who is impacted? In government, and large organisations the financial risk is born by the organisation, not the individual. Thus, financial risks and decisions can be far easier to take without real research and testing. This can and does result in many corporate or government decisions that fail, have massive cost blowouts, or in a worse-case scenario end up in insolvency. The risks that individuals face in these scenarios are career risks from which they can often recover.

So, Let's Look at How to Make Considered and Informed Decisions

Define The Problem Clearly

Identify The Root Issue: Don't focus solely on symptoms, ask "why" repeatedly to get to the heart of the problem you're trying to solve. As we have already identified, communication is a symptom of what can be a variety of issues. In most cases they will be found in the organisational culture, but behind this again could likely be leader behaviour. It's like trying to find the primary source of a river that might need travelling up every tributary.

Specify Your Goals: Be clear about what you want to achieve with your decision and define tangible results.

Understand The Context: Consider the wider situation or bigger picture, any constraints, and how this decision relates to overall plans or objectives.

Gather Information and Perspectives

Avoid Tunnel Vision: Seek data, research, and input from various sources, internal and external. This could include experts, stakeholders, past experiences, or even past competitors.

Challenge Assumptions: Question your own biases and those of others. Are there assumptions being made that need to be re-evaluated? I've looked at bad decisions made in many corporate clients, and analysed why they got it so wrong. In almost every case the answer was in the assumptions that were made in the decision process. The assumptions related to markets both output and input, government and competitor behaviour, currency changes, energy, innovation, social upheaval and climate. These are just a few of the influencing areas. This is why I have emphasised the need for a systems approach where all the organisation's environmental factors that can come into play are considered.

Open The Floor: Encourage diverse perspectives from people on your team, those who will be affected by the decision, and other people in your industry or related industries.

Gathering and Evaluating

Brainstorm Creatively: Get a multidisciplinary and melting-pot team together to maximise input. Generate a wide range of possibilities, without immediately criticising any of them. Encourage wild ideas as they can sometimes spark more practical solutions. This can be not only a fun and stimulating activity for the participants, but also a great team building activity. You need to do this in a professional way, so first read about the best process to get the best results.

Assess Pros and Cons: Carefully weigh the benefits and drawbacks of each option against your desired outcomes and priorities. This can be a valuable part of the brainstorming process.

Consider Risks and Contingencies: Along with the assumptions made, these are areas where failure to effectively consider them can result in things going pear shaped very easily. What are potential negative outcomes and where could the Law of Unintended Consequences come into play? Again, you can include this in brainstorming sessions.

Don't Over Analyse: I'm reminded of a very successful merchant banker who said. "We don't invest in projects requiring long-winded, and time-consuming evaluation before making a decision. We make immediate investments in projects clearly showing real prospects of success".

Decide, and Own It

The Power of Intuition: While a data-driven approach is critical, don't discount your gut feeling. If something seems off, even if you can't pinpoint exactly why, you can still factor it in. In my experience "gut feeling" has proven on several occasions to be the feeling I should have followed. In recent years there has been a remarkable amount of research showing the profound two-way influence of traffic between the brain and the gut. This has supported my entirely unscientific belief I've held for years, that a "gut feeling" is in fact a "brain feeling" that results from years of conscious and subconscious learning, as well as some primeval input.

Make The Call: After due consideration and evaluation, pick the option that aligns best with your goals and feels like the right direction. Be bold and take ownership of the decision recognising than in everyone there is a risk. If you have done your homework well, risk will be at a minimum.

Avoid Second-Guessing: Protracted self-doubt or cognitive dissonance post decision can occur, and lead to second guessing or inaction. Own your decision and act to achieve your planned outcome.

Communicate and Execute: Bring key stakeholders along with you. Be transparent and articulate with sound reasoning and rationale.

Monitor and Adjust: Remain flexible and assess how the decision is playing out. Don't be afraid to adapt or change course as this may become necessary.

Extra Tips

Beware of Decision Fatigue: Avoid making major decisions when burnt-out or under stress, as alertness and mental energy are essential for clear thinking.

Time Frame Matters: Urgent decisions sometimes require swift action on incomplete information and is where experience in decision making can prove invaluable. At other times allowing a problem to "incubate" can lead to better outcomes.

Learn From Experience: Each decision, whether successful or not, brings lessons to refine your judgement and your decision process in the future.

We can't leave decision making without a bit of associated humour.

Committees: The Black Holes of Decisions

Minutes are scrupulously recorded while hours are mercilessly lost in a time warp. Participants emerge bleary eyed, unsure if anything was actually accomplished.

Every committee requires a designated contrarian, whose role involves disagreeing in principle with any suggestion, thus ensuring endless healthy debate.

Success of a committee is measured inversely to the number of decisions actually made.

The committee of infinite decision. Too many cooks spoil the broth. Even simple decisions face an endless cycle of review and approval by countless committees, stalling any progress.

Schools Of Decision-Making

The Ostrich Approach: heads buried firmly in the sand; all contrary data is ignored. Ideal when impending doom is inconvenient to the current agenda.

The Lemming Method: Everyone enthusiastically charges in the same direction, mostly off a cliff. High levels of participation and a strong sense of team spirit are trademarks of this approach.

The Weather-Vane Technique: Opinions shift expertly with whoever is speaking the loudest at the time. Useful for those aspiring to high levels of management.

The Magpie Initiative: Shiny new ideas are endlessly pursued, regardless of relevance or **practicality**. It's characterised by the excessive use of buzzwords and a sense of frantic activity masking a lack of actual progress.

The PowerPoint Process: All critical thinking is pummelled into submission by slides crammed with unreadable charts and inspirational stock photos.

The Devious Deploy: For leaders who surreptitiously outsource their decision making to incognizant (not incontinent) consultants who they can blame when everything goes haywire.

Beware Organisational Anarchists

We need to be aware of organisational deviant behaviours, including those of sociopaths, that can put our organisation at risk. Let's look at a guide or framework for recognising them.

Spectrum of Severity: From simple malfeasance to outright sabotage, we need to look at degrees of deviance, especially where mostly harmless isn't harmless. Sociopathic behaviours, micro aggressions or passive-aggressive tactics can rapidly erode a positive culture. This was evident in the cases I've described. We need to look for red flags.

Seeing the Red Flags: Changes in employee behaviour, work patterns, absenteeism, staff turnover or attitudes warrant closer attention.

Performance Dips: Understand how sudden shifts in productivity or quality standards can signal underlying issues.

Decoding the Whispers: Create safe channels for confidential reporting, along with a "see-something: say-something" culture but not one fuelling gossip.

Dangers of a Toxic System: Bureaucracy can breed monsters. Complex environments with vague accountability, pressure cooker deadlines, and lack of consequences can all promote risky corner cutting or buck passing.

Balancing Justice and Protection: Develop a framework for fair and transparent investigations.

Avoid Knee-Jerk Reactions: Thoughtful and fair due process should be seen as appropriate and fair by all and in the immediate and long-term interests of the organisation.

The Human Factor: Stress, supervisory behaviour, personal hardship, family issues and feeling under-appreciated or under-rewarded, can all result in deviant behaviours. These are largely avoided in cultures where people really are prioritised, and their circumstances known. On quite a few occasions in organisations I asked group members to write down what they knew of their work mates, and colleagues with whom they interacted and their circumstances. With few exceptions it was very little despite mission statements saying, "our people are our priority".

Prevention or Cure: As with every problem we look at, prevention is invariably easier and less costly than a cure. This is where instilling strong values and ethics, really knowing and listening to your people, recognising when they have issues, and addressing them, substantially mitigates the risks of aberrant behaviour damaging the organisation.

The Spectrum of Criminal Influence

Beyond Mobster Movies: Dispelling stereotypes, to recognise the breadth of criminal activity affecting companies. This can be from petty theft to sophisticated cyber-crime, with the criminals ranging from individuals to governments. Courtesy of the internet the latter seem almost invariably to be in distant countries, with little or no capacity to act or implement reprisal against them.

External Threats: Organisations whether government, public or private have, since they first existed, been targets for conspirators or criminals. This has dramatically increased since the inception of the internet. Organisations must deal with increasing threats of cyber invasions, disruption, warfare and theft, potentially on a massive scale. Not only is this threat from conventional criminals for profit and cash payments, but from foreign governments and corporations. Both can be seeking to obtain design, manufacturing or other secrets from corporations. Governments are often also seeking military, defence, economic, social or other vital data.

Internal Threats: We can find employees guilty of theft, not just of money but patent or proprietary designs or systems, embezzlement and data breaches. The latter may well be sold to competitors or foreign governments.

Grey Areas: We also commonly see business practices that skirt legality. These can be aggressive competition and sales behaviour, or unethical processes and breaches of legislation or regulations with uninformed victims. Corporate examples that I have seen, in companies with whom I have been associated, were blatant espionage. In one case a manager in our company applied for and got a senior job with a major competitor. He stayed in this role while reporting back everything he learned including the sales and marketing strategy and programmes, new product developments, as well as accounting and finance information. His colleagues, me included, were all envious of his situation. Not only was he was earning two very nice incomes, but what he had learnt from our competitor put him in the plum seat for promotion on his return. The second example was very similar but a lighter shade of grey! The chief executive of a large private engineering company applied for and was interviewed for the chief executive role, in a larger publicly listed competitor company. In the final selection process, he was made aware of the public company corporate plans. These even included the potential acquisition of the private company he worked for. He was offered the job as chief executive but declined, as the whole application had just been a ploy to learn what a competitor planned, and how you could get a competitive advantage. There were some very red faces and concerns for careers when this all came out!

The issues that governments, companies and even individuals face, has increasingly led to the recognition of the need for serious risk management strategies, and defence actions. It is a war!

Apart from competitor strategies such as those just described its worth mentioning a few more points of vulnerability and mitigation actions.

Physical Assets: Identify weak points in security that can allow for theft of products, equipment or sensitive information. For example, there are some major utilities in Australia that use 110volt tools and equipment that won't work with the normal 220volt power supply. Others block the ability to download data from computer systems or record any such activity.

Digital Fortresses: Mapping IT vulnerabilities, understanding where attacks like ransomware or data breaches can find weaknesses.

The Human Factor: Social engineering, bribery, coercion or simple employee opportunism. Criminals can target employees and exploit trusting relationships. Beware ultra loyal employees who never take holidays. I was amazed at the number of such totally trusted persons, stealing large sums over extended periods, who I discovered while engaged in consulting assignments.

Supply Chain Blind Spots: This is one of the big areas of risk and financial loss for companies. I've seen numerous examples involving purchasing officers and have even had attempts to bribe me to award contracts. These are particularly common where time has a very high cost, such as in construction projects of almost any kind. The military is renowned for this, as are mining companies. I'll just describe two. One in a major mining house where on one contract alone, the purchasing officer was receiving $12000 per month black money. His salary was $20000 a year, and you could buy a nice home for $60,000. So not at all bad! He was ultimately sacked, but not charged, as it would have proved very embarrassing. He went to another mining house to do the same thing! He had already bought a lovely home in a top beach suburb as well as cars and a sixteen-metre cabin cruiser!

The second is a multinational oil company. In this case I was contacted by a friend who was the owner and managing director of a large structural engineering company. Recently he had received a request to tender on upgrading service stations for a major oil company. He later had a phone call from the chief purchasing officer of the oil company. In it he advised that they would in fact be progressively upgrading 800-1000 service stations. Further, he advised my friend that if he tendered within a given price range, a percentage of which would be for the purchasing officer, he could be assured of getting the contract. He was ringing me to ask what I thought he should do, as he could make a very substantial profit, but was concerned with the morality. I simply said that I'm no moral guardian, but if you don't accept, someone else will and on the same terms, so I'd accept. He did, and he was ultimately able to retire on that contract, bought a lovely property on acreage, a yacht, and lived happily ever after.

No matter the size of the company you absolutely need to have systems to ensure that purchasing procedures are routinely tested for integrity.

Red Flags. Changes in patterns of behaviour, changes or abnormalities in financial data, unexplained losses or profit reduction, whispers of unethical activity, noticeable new expenditure by staff on assets or activities.

The Culture Factor: Does your organisation prioritize compliance or is there pressure to cut corners or expedite things, as this is ripe for exploitation.

Internal Collusion: This is where two or more employees become complicit in criminal activity. It can be very hard to discover and correct and is where routines to assess integrity of operations, such as role and responsibility changes are essential.

The Fallout: Beyond immediate or longer-term financial loss there can be serious collateral damage to reputation, legal consequences, erosion of trust and loss of good staff.

Risk Assessment: It is not about paranoia but a deliberate process of identifying vulnerabilities specific to your industry and location.

Multilayered Security: Physical and digital policies and systems that promote safe reporting of concerns that may include firewalls and whistleblowing.

Education and Cooperation: Employees at all levels should understand threats and be empowered to speak up as the first line of defence. At the corporate level collaboration with law enforcement and industry groups, learning of threat intelligence is a wise move.

Response and Recovery: Prepare in advance for a breach or incident, knowing essential contacts, and steps to preserve evidence of means, methods and suspects.

Damage Control and lessons learned: This requires transparent handling of the situation, internal reviews and actions implemented to prevent recurrence.

Reviewing the Use of Consultants

We have looked at using consultants before. Using consultants can absolutely offer benefits to organisations, but it's essential to be aware of the potential dangers and pitfalls involved, so here's a breakdown. Before engaging consultants make sure that your reference checks go beyond the basics. Don't settle for standard reference calls. Ask probing questions about the challenges that arose during the consultant's previous engagements, how they overcame them, and whether the results matched or exceeded their client's expectations.

Dependency Risk: Over reliance on consultants can hinder internal skill development. Organisations may forget how to strategically solve their own problems without getting constant external input.

Knowledge Drain: When consultants leave, they take valuable project-specific knowledge with them. Inadequate documentation or knowledge transfer leaves the organisation in the lurch.

Cost Escalation: Consultant fees can quickly balloon, especially with unforeseen project scope changes, hidden costs, or long-term reliance. The ROI, return on investment, may not justify the expense.

Implementation and Cultural Gaps: Consultants may provide brilliant recommendations, but they might clash with the company's internal capabilities, budget, or existing work culture, making implementation a nightmare.

Disrupting Internal Dynamics: Employees can feel resentful or threatened by outsiders coming in and suggesting changes, especially if communication from leadership is poor. This could even result in the loss of good staff.

Misaligned Incentives: We have looked at this before. Consultants are ultimately concerned with their billable hours and project milestones, potentially leading them to propose solutions that aren't truly in the best long in term interests of the company.

Misunderstanding the Landscape: Consultants may lack the same depth of insight into your company culture, history, and internal politics as employees do. This can be mitigated by creating detailed briefs about your organisation, include pain points, past failures, and potential internal resistant areas. Involve key stakeholders in the process.

Recommending Overly Complex Solutions: Some consultants feel pressured to justify their value with elaborate strategies. These may be unrealistic for your organisation's capabilities. To mitigate this, emphasise practicality and the need for simple implementation in your initial briefing. Demand realistic budgets and timelines from the start.

Failure to Deliver: There is always a risk of consultants promises exceeding their ability to deliver. To mitigate this outcome, breakdown the project into smaller, measurable milestones. Include checkpoints and potential exit clauses in the contract to be actioned if performance is persistently unsatisfactory.

Organisational Miscellanea

The Fine Art of Looking Busy

Masterful Inbox Juggle: When the boss walks by, furiously click between multiple email and spreadsheet threads with furrowed brows. Content is irrelevant; the illusion of intense work is critical.

Strategic Walk and Talk: Urgent-looking stroll down the hallway with a single sheet of paper. Purposeful stride suggests critical mission, yet the contents could be last week's lunch order.

Keyboard Mashing Concert: Burst into sudden typing flurries when anyone appears behind you. Emails that were languishing moments ago require a rapid flurry of activity.

Inevitable Elements of Bureaucracy

The Unfindable Form: There is a form for everything, some with multiple copies, but locating the right one requires an archaeological expedition through outdated intranet folders and the wisdom of one employee who has been there for millennia.

Approval Chain Labyrinth: Getting a simple idea approved requires navigating a maze of signoffs from managers, their managers and that vaguely threatening person in Compliance, whose name nobody knows.

Mandatory "Optional" Training: Sessions labelled as "optional" mysteriously become mandatory the day before, accompanied by vague but dire warnings about unspecified consequences of non-participation.

Meetings Gone Mad

The Endless Status Update: A two-hour meeting dedicated to reviewing progress that could have been communicated in a five-line email.

Could've Been an Email Award: Meetings called without an agenda, purpose, or any semblance of a goal, destined to end, with the collective realisation that no one knows why they are there. However, there is a collective agreement that time was effectively wasted.

Recurring Purgatory: Meetings for the sake of having meetings-usually the same update repeated week after week.

Talkers are going to Talk: Some people just love the sound of their own voice. They will derail discussions with irrelevant tangents, dominating the room while accomplishing nothing.

Tech Troubles: The dreaded "can you hear me now?" loop, screen share fails, and those 15 minutes figuring out who has the mute button on, sets the tone!

Death by PowerPoint: Slides packed with miniscule text, read verbatim by a presenter with the charisma of a wet paper bag. Need I say more? Yes, I must! As the presenter further excites the participants by saying he only has 48 more slides!

The Circular Argument: Two or more people locked in a debate that repeats the same points over and over, going nowhere.

The Sidetracked Special: When what started as a budget discussion somehow morphs into a debate on the morning tea break policy and will there still be biscuits.

The Never-Ending Story: The 30-minute scheduled meeting somehow drags on for 2 hours, leaving everyone drained and resentful.

The Ghost Town: Half the attendees don't show, those who do have no clue why they are there, and everyone is waiting for whatever it is they are there for to be over soon.

The Decision That Isn't: After all the talk, no decision gets made, and you plan another meeting to discuss why the meeting ended with no decision!

The Beautiful Consensus: Time has been taken, everything debated at length, and we have achieved consensus despite everyone being very to vaguely concerned and dissatisfied with the outcome.

How to limit Meeting Insanity

Ruthless Agendas: Distribute beforehand only to essential people, stick to them and appoint someone to keep things on track.

Could This be An Email: Seriously ask this question before calling a meeting.

Time Limits: Set them on topics and talkers and enforce them.

Action Items, not Just Talk: Every meeting should end with clear action steps, time- lines and those responsible for achieving them.

Workplace "Logic"

Technology Paradox: Enforcing strict password policies involving obscure symbols and frequent changes, while still using outdated legacy software from distant decades.

Cost-Saving Obsession: Micromanaging office supply spending and telephone usage while executives jet off for a "corporate team-building retreat" at an exclusive resort.

Innovation, But Make It Familiar: Investing heavily in trendy words like "synergy", "disruption" and "ground-breaking" while maintaining the same rigid and unproductive work processes in place for decades.

If it Ain't Broke Don't Fix it: Even if it's incredibly slow, inefficient and makes everyone want to scream.

Thoughtful Change: To encourage collaboration, we are moving everyone into an open floor plan where it's impossible to concentrate.

Paradoxical Promotion: "You are so good at your job; we're promoting you to a position where you will have no idea what you are doing". The Peter Principle in Action!

Why Don't We Finish with a Hitchhikers Guide to Being a Great Communicator

But first some reflections on communication we frequently encounter.

We're not on the same page, we are not even in the same library.

I'm not ignoring you. I'm selectively filtering your input.

It's as clear as a wink to a blind bat!

Your email went straight into my brains spam folder!

It's like we are speaking a different language....and I don't mean English and French!

Autocorrect changed it! Really!

Did that meeting invite disappear into your calendar black hole?

The Wisdom of Confusion

If you can't explain it simply, you probably don't understand it yourself.

Sometimes the best response to confusing situation is just to nod and smile like you're in on a secret joke.

When all else fails, blame it on technology. It works, even if it's not true.

Getting a Bit More Serious

Know Your Destination: Before you start talking, emailing, or presenting. Be clear on your objective. What information do you need to convey? What decision or outcome are you hoping for?

Adapt To the Local Dialect: Every team, department, and organisation have their own communication styles. Are they brief and results focused, or do they value relationship building small talk? Mirror their style to build rapport.

Adapt To the Language: Different teams and departments can have their own languages. Finance, sales and IT all have specialised vocabulary. You may have to learn it!

Master the Universal Translator: Focus on clarity and simplicity. Avoid jargon and acronyms that might not be understood. Explain complex concepts in a way anyone could grasp.

Listen With More Than Just Your Ears: Great communication is a two-way street. A dialogue and not a monologue. Pay attention to body language, tone of voice and what is *not* being said as much as the actual words.

Don't Fail on Follow Up: Follow up on important conversations, especially if action items are involved. Summarise decisions and next steps to ensure everyone is on the same page.

Always Carry a Phrasebook: A few well-chosen phrases at the ready can be lifesavers: "Can you elaborate on that"? "let me summarise to make sure I understand", "I hear your concerns, let's explore some solutions together".

Upgrade Your Empathy: Truly understanding your audience, their needs, concerns, and priorities, makes your communication far more effective.

Finally-Don't Panic: Staying calm and composed increases your credibility as a communicator, even when delivering difficult news.

I hope this Earth Edition of The Hitchhiker's Workbook and Toolbox helps you set course and follow a trajectory to get you to your destination safely at warp speed with a few smiles, a few diversions and without too many hazards along the way.

And Thank You for All the Experiences

FIN

www.ingramcontent.com/pod-product-compliance
Lightning Source LLC
Chambersburg PA
CBHW071207210326
41597CB00016B/1714